Spectacular Support Centers

As useful as a Swiss Army knife for any small to medium call center manager whether veteran or newbie: This is your guide. As a must-have in one's library, it'll be one of your most worn-out references in your career. It is practical and very illustrative in its approach to solving common call center/IT help desk issues. Bravo!

Richard Brannock, Director,
Americas Technical Assistance
Center, Check Point Software
Technologies

Spectacular Support Centers is an easy-to-read and invaluable guide for service managers. It covers everything that a help desk/support center manager needs to know to effectively run the organization. Not only does it cover every aspect of the support center, but it also provides practical examples that can be applied within your operation. Kristin's vast experience in the technology service industry is captured in this book, a must-read for managers of both small and large support operations.

John Hamilton, President,
Service Strategies Corporation

Kristin Robertson continues to share her expertise with the support industry through Spectacular Support Centers. This book is full of great advice and examples to help new support center managers and those managing smaller support centers improve the quality of their services.

Rick Joslin, HDI Executive Director
of Certification & Training

This is the A to Z of small help desk best practices. Kristin has included everything. Her knowledge and experience come together in an easy-to-read book that even the most seasoned help desk manager will benefit from. I know this book will be a resource I will refer to often while running my support center.

Nathan Harvey, Manager, Tech
Support, FedEx Kinko's

This book is a "must-read" for the smaller support center manager, with great practical advice on establishing a "best-in-class" customer support center.

Scott Stegner, Director of Global
Product Support, TAC

D1104239

I've been looking for a book like this for years. This is the only book I have found that directly addresses the needs of my smaller support center. This book won't end up on my bookshelf; it will stay right on my desk for quick access.

> Douglas Coco, Support Center
> Manager, Mohawk Industries, and
> President, DFW Chapter, HDI

I found Kristin Robertson's Spectacular Support Centers *to be very comprehensive yet also very easy to read and understand. She is able to condense an amazing amount of valuable information into a relatively small volume. While it focuses on the smaller support centers, it is valuable for support centers of any size.*

> Terry Allen, Support Center
> Consultant, Past President of HDI's
> DFW Chapter, Past Director of HDI's
> Central Region and Member of HDI
> Member Advisory Board

Small support operations is where it's at in today's entrepreneurial economy, and Kristin's approach is helping new entrepreneurs to drive efficiency and manage the growth of their remote service operations. [This is] the success roadmap for managers of small technical support operations.

> Ben Stephens, Principal/Vice President,
> Service Strategies

Here is the roadmap for success within a small support organization.

> Dan Wilson, General Manager,
> PMV Technologies

Spectacular Support Centers *is sure to become THE guidebook for all smaller support centers. [It is] packed full of insightful commentary, useful diagrams and helpful metrics, and anyone in the support center industry can learn from Kristin Robertson's expertise. If you are new to support center leadership, this book will provide the basis to build your support center around. If you're an experienced leader, this book will provide you with the framework upon which to improve your team.*

> Phil Gerbyshak, Help Desk Manager,
> author of *10 Ways to Make It Great!*
> and editor of HelpDeskNotes.com

Spectacular Support Centers

Best Practices for Small to Mid-Sized Help Desks
and Technical Support Centers

Spectacular Support Centers

Best Practices for Small to Mid-Sized Help Desks
and Technical Support Centers

Kristin E. Robertson

Library of Congress Control Number: 2007901996

Robertson, Kristin E.

[1. Information Technology – Management 2. Customer Service –
Management]

ISBN 0971340692

Customer Service Press
Bolton, MA

Table of Contents

Preface

Smaller support centers are the Rodney Dangerfields of the industry – they don't get no respect. This segment of the market is underserved at conferences and in support center literature. The greatest proportion of support centers today have fewer than 75 analysts (mid-sized centers), and an even greater proportion of centers have fewer than 20 analysts (small centers). Fortunately, vendors in the support center industry have targeted this growing segment of the market for years.

No two ways about it, though: Smaller support centers have more fun. The smaller support center has the opportunity to create more job diversity for its analysts, it can forge stronger, more intimate relationships with customers and it can create a more cohesive team environment. In addition, smaller supports are generally more nimble than larger ones, as they are not constrained by multiple layers of management and the need for strict adherence to processes. Smaller centers can be spectacular!

If your support center is small to mid-sized, this book is for you. It is for you whether you manage an internal help desk where customers are employees of the company, or an external product support center that serves customers of your company. Because internal and external support centers are slightly different, there are clearly marked sections in this book that designate recommendations for internal support centers and external support centers.

"Best practices" is a common term today. It reflects the fact that the support industry has matured to the point that we know what works and what does not – most of what you can imagine doing in a support center has already been tried, and it either worked or didn't. Best practices build on that collective body of experience and show us proven ways to run a support center. Please note that we always refer to best practices in the plural, meaning there is not just one right way to perform a process, but several variations to choose from, according to the support center's environment. In this book, we focus on the process variations that work for small to mid-sized support organizations.

I wrote this book because I once managed a small support center that grew to be a mid-sized support center. I was constantly searching for appropriate resources for my support center and often felt overwhelmed by the "big guys" at conferences, local industry meetings and vendor fairs. The support tools they could afford were a mere fantasy for my lean budget, and the processes they employed were too formal and inappropriate for the intimate confines of my 15-person support center. With this book, and its easily accessible information on all facets of small to mid-sized support centers, I feel confident you won't have the same frustrations I did.

I also have managed large support centers. This may not seem relevant at first blush, but in order to understand how to use best practices for the smaller center, it is important to understand how large centers work.

In my consulting practice, I have been fortunate to work with support centers of all sizes and shapes, including internal help desks, hardware tech support departments and software support centers. I enjoy them all, but my heart is in the smaller support centers.

As a faculty member of HDI University (formerly known as Help Desk Institute) and an auditor for the Service Capability & Performance (SCP) Support Standard site certification program created by Service Strategies Corporation, I am in a strong position to understand best practices in the support center industry. I teach best practices and advise clients about best practices every day. I look forward to imparting some of this knowledge to you.

Acknowledgements

Many people have helped to make this book a reality. I am so appreciative of my review board of practitioners – Douglas Coco, Robin Rea, Nathan Harvey, Dan Wilson and Phil Gerbyshak – who read the book and offered thoughtful suggestions. Special thanks to Terry Allen, who read the manuscript thoroughly and provided insightful and thought-provoking comments. Thanks to my assistant, Laura Armbruster, and my editor, Anita Robeson, who held my hand through many publishing adventures. My husband, Adam Gordon, and my two teenaged children, Eric and Rebecca, deserve mention for suffering through the long days of writing and editing. My dear friends Therese Adamiec and Elizabeth Vise and my business coach, Jayne Gardner, provided the encouragement and support that only good friends can.

Lastly, I owe a deep bow of gratitude to the entire support center community, including my clients, my friends at Service Strategies and those at HDI. I have learned everything I know from my experiences in this industry and through my associations with the many fine people in it.

Respectfully,
Kristin Robertson
Colleyville, Texas
www.krconsulting.com
February 2007

Terminology Used

The wording used in this book was chosen to be inclusive of both internal support centers and external support centers. Information Technology Infrastructure Library (ITIL) terminology is not consistently used in this book because external support centers are generally not concerned with this set of best practices. Therefore, it is important to understand the following terms and their equivalents.

Terms used in this book	Equivalents
Support center	• Service desk • Help desk • Technical support • Product support
Support request	• Service request • Incident • Call • Contact • Ticket • Case • Issue • Work order
Analyst	• Representative • Agent • Professional • Technician • Specialist
First-level	• Frontline
Senior analyst	• Mentor • Team lead • Second-level • Experts
Contact	• Call • Email • Electronic support request
Service management system	• Call tracking system • Ticket tracking system • Request management system • Incident management system • Problem management system • Customer relationship management system • Support system

## CHAPTER ONE

Strategic Leadership

LEADERSHIP IS THE ART OF GUIDING a group of people in a certain direction or toward a goal. Strategy is typically defined as a plan to achieve stated goals, but another layer of the word's meaning implies that strategy involves plans that affect the financial well-being of a company or organization. Strategic leadership, therefore, is the art of leading with a view toward the financial implications of the direction taken. Support center managers must balance the need to provide outstanding technical support with the strategic and financial aims of the company. This can be a tremendous balancing act.

In the internal support center environment, Information Technology Service Management (ITSM), an approach to IT leadership that emphasizes aligning the IT organization with the business, mandates this balancing. This used to be a novel concept, but today any IT manager who is not supporting the needs of the business is probably not a candidate for long-term employment. The Information Technology Infrastructure Library (ITIL) is a framework that enables the ITSM goal of aligning IT with the business. ITIL best practices are incorporated into this book.

Mission Statement

The adage "If you don't know where you are going, any road will take you" is useful for any organization, including support centers. Creating a mission statement defines the destination of the support center. There is ample material written on how to write a mission statement. An Internet search can identify those resources.

The smaller support center must keep in mind that its mission statement must align with the mission statements of the corporation and the IT department (if applicable). Meaning and content should flow downward from the corporate mission statement and objectives. A mission statement should include the purpose of the support center, the business value of the services provided and descriptions of the level or type of support provided.

A second consideration is that the mission should be designed using a team effort – all analysts should be involved in its creation. One way to develop a mission statement with the support team is to present the background of a mission statement in a team meeting, emphasizing the importance of aligning with corporate statements and values. Then, ask the support analysts to contribute ideas, phrases and outcomes for a mission statement. Commission a small group of analysts to gather all the ideas offered and wordsmith the statement. Periodically review the group's progress to make sure it is on track, in terms of both deadlines and the alignment of its work with corporate mission, values and objectives. Present the final draft of the statement to small groups within the support center, incorporate edits and create the final version.

The adage "If you don't know where you are going, any road will take you" is useful for any organization, including support centers.

If the mission statement is not an important part of the support center's daily life, the creation effort has been a waste of time. To make a mission statement relevant, it has to be a living, useful document. Managers should be constantly referring to it as a litmus test for decision-making. If a course of action does not support the mission, it should not be undertaken. One way to remind people of the mission is to frame and display the mission statement prominently in the support center. Some support centers post their mission statement as the screen saver on each person's computer. Managers should regularly refer to the mission statement in group meetings.

Goals and Objectives

The best way for support centers to align themselves with the business is for managers to consciously seek out the business's objectives and adopt goals that support them. A best practice is for the support center to create yearly goals and objectives that cascade from the corporation's overall objectives. Cascading refers to the many levels of goals that might be set in an organization, starting with the top or corporate goals and flowing down the organizational chart to departments and then individuals. Typically, a corporation's objectives include profitability, sales and customer retention targets, new product introduction goals, and internal goals such as creating a supportive work environment. After corporate goals are

The best practice is to create yearly goals and objectives that cascade from the corporation's overall objectives.

established, the support center creates overall goals for the group. Finally, individual analyst's goals are created. It is important that all levels be in alignment. This process has the obvious advantage of ensuring that all departments are clear on what is important to the future health of the corporation and that all individuals are marching toward the same destination.

Here is an example of cascading goals for an external support center:

Goals for an External Support Center

Corporate objective	Increase customer loyalty.	Improve shareholder value (increase revenues, reduce expenses).	Create a workplace that is best-in-class.	Produce products that are feature-rich, dependable and cost-effective.
Support center objectives	Improve customer satisfaction scores; improve response times; improve first contact resolution rates.	Increase first contact resolution (saves money); increase adoption of self-service offerings; increase support contract renewal rate; improve reporting to sales of customer support requests.	Improve scheduling of analysts; initiate an employee survey within support center; provide stress management classes; provide team-building events; improve educational offerings for analysts.	Strengthen development liaison position; increase support's role in product development life cycle.
Analyst objectives	Improve personal customer satisfaction scores; improve personal first contact resolution rates.	Attend technical training; increase personal use of knowledge base; encourage each caller to visit the support web site.	Attend stress management training; complete employee survey; serve on celebrations team.	Attend all development meetings for my product.

Goals for an internal support center might be slightly different. In this case, the IT department is involved and has goals of its own, adding another layer of cascades. The internal support center's customers are employees of the company, so the focus must be on keeping employees productive and on improving systems availability. In addition, the IT department is there to support the evolving technology needs of each customer-facing department. On page 6 is an example of cascading goals for an internal support center.

Financial Leadership

Financial leadership is all about being a good steward of corporate or institutional money and making good decisions about investments in the support center. Although an in-depth discussion of financial matters is outside the scope of this book, the basics will be covered here.

The most important equation in capitalism is:

Revenues – expenses = profits

Every organization, including non-profits and government entities, has to be aware of this equation; after all, if expenses exceed revenues, the organization loses money. Negative consequences such as lay-offs, plant closures and even the bankruptcy of an organization may follow. The same applies to personal finance – if you spend more money than you make, negative consequences can include credit card debt and, ultimately, personal bankruptcy.

To increase profits, organizations can either increase revenues or decrease expenses.

To increase profits, organizations can either increase revenues or decrease expenses. By revenues, we mean money coming in from outside the corporation, not internal charge-backs. Internal support centers, because they serve internal customers and do not generate

Cascading Goals for an Internal Support Center

Corporate objective	Increase customer loyalty.	Increase sales, reduce costs.	Create a workplace that is best-in-class.
IT depart-ment goals	Enhance CRM systems to enable customer-facing departments to serve customers; work with business units to create systems to meas-ure loyalty.	Enhance ERP system to improve production rates and reduce cycle times; increase internal customers' productivity by increasing systems availability and reduc-ing downtime and by introducing mobile computing.	Ensure training plans are completed; implement employee satisfaction surveys; improve inter-departmental communications; enforce OLA commitments.
Support center objectives	Work with sales to create new SLA; create customer training program for new systems; conduct brown bag lunch training sessions on mini-topics for sales and service departments.	Increase first contact resolution (saves money); increase adoption of self-service offerings; report resolution times versus SLA targets; improve customer satisfaction scores; improve response times.	Improve scheduling of analysts; initiate an employee survey within support center; provide stress management classes; provide team-building events; improve educational offerings for analysts.
Analyst objectives	Create four mini-training sessions for customers.	Improve personal customer satisfaction scores; improve personal first contact resolution rates; increase personal use of knowledge base; encourage each caller to visit the support web site.	Attend technical training; attend stress management training; complete employee survey; serve on celebrations team.

revenue, can usually only decrease expenses in order to affect prof-its. Occasionally there is an exception to this rule, such as when an internal support center generates revenue by becoming an out-sourcer and offering its services to outside companies.

External support centers exert a bit more influence over the revenue stream of the company. According to a research study from the Association of Support Professionals, over half of software companies' revenues now come from support-related services, including maintenance support and upgrades.[1] Even with the ability to influence more than half the company's revenues, most external support centers are under tremendous pressure to reduce expenses and make support more efficient.

Most support centers operate as a cost center, which means they are not allocated any revenues. Profit centers, on the other hand, show both revenues and expenses on their financial reporting. Whether the support center is a cost or a profit center, the principle financial instrument that managers create and manage is a budget. The budget is a projection that lists, line by line, the anticipated revenues (if applicable) and expenses of the support center. It is generally created before the beginning of the fiscal year.

The chart on page 9 is an example of a fictitious support center's budget.

This budget shows projected expenses (note there are no revenues reported for this support center) for the entire year, month by month. The manager of this center would receive monthly and quarterly reports from the finance team on how the support center is doing compared to the budget.

One important financial calculation that even small support centers find handy is the cost per call or cost per contact. If you are able to generate a budget such as the one on page 9, it is easy to figure this important metric. Simply divide the total annual number of contacts received into the support center's total expenses. If the support center whose budget is shown on page 9 received 40,978 support requests that year, the cost per contact is about $30, as follows:

[1] *Association of Support Professionals, Maintenance & Services Ratios / 2006, www.asponline.com (Membership may be needed to access the report.)*

Total expenses	$1,224,567
Total support requests	40,978
Expenses/# of support requests	$29.88
Cost per contact	$29.88

As we shall see in later chapters, the cost per contact can be helpful in quantifying the costs of defects. It is also a useful number in building cost justifications for purchasing new support technology. It is, however, an advanced metric that is impossible for some centers to calculate.

Many small support center managers are handicapped in their ability to understand the financial impact of their decisions. This is because the support center's budget is included in another manager's budget and cannot easily be separated out. Typically in IT support centers, the budget responsibility is kept at a higher level, perhaps at the IT director or CIO level because it does not make sense to ask finance people to create reports for a small support center. Small external support centers often have the same challenge – their budget numbers are included in a larger group's reporting and cannot be broken out. Even in these cases, the support manager can be mindful of monetary issues. Keeping in mind the basic formula of capitalism, the support manager needs to understand that anything that increases expenses, such as hiring more analysts, buying new support tools or increasing training, must be justified.

Justifying a purchase or an increase in expenses is a financial concept that every support manager needs to understand.

Justifying a purchase or an increase in expenses is a financial concept that every support manager needs to understand. The way you justify an increase in expenses is to show that some benefit will

	January	Feb	March	April	May	June	July	August	Sept	Oct	Nov	Dec	TOTAL
Staff salaries	$61,780	$61,780	$61,780	$61,780	$61,780	$61,780	$64,869	$64,869	$64,869	$64,869	$64,869	$64,869	$759,894
Incentive bonuses	$2,500	$0	$0	$2,500	$0	$0	$2,500	$0	$0	$2,500	$0	$5,000	$15,000
Employee benefits	$12,253	$12,253	$12,253	$12,253	$12,253	$12,253	$12,253	$12,253	$12,253	$12,253	$12,253	$12,253	$150,276
Training costs	$2,782	$2,782	$2,782	$2,782	$2,782	$2,782	$2,782	$2,782	$2,782	$2,782	$2,782	$2,782	$33,384
Office space	$6,689	$6,689	$6,689	$6,689	$6,689	$6,689	$6,689	$6,689	$6,689	$6,689	$6,689	$6,689	$80,268
Office furniture	$767	$767	$767	$767	$767	$767	$767	$767	$767	$767	$767	$767	$9,204
Utilities	$1,092	$988	$861	$861	$769	$861	$899	$955	$861	$789	$899	$979	$10,814
Office supplies	$212	$212	$212	$212	$212	$212	$212	$212	$212	$212	$212	$212	$2,544
Hardware	$4,991	$4,991	$4,991	$4,991	$4,991	$4,991	$4,991	$4,991	$4,991	$4,991	$4,991	$4,991	$59,892
Software	$692	$692	$692	$692	$692	$692	$692	$692	$692	$692	$692	$692	$8,304
Support/maintenance contracts	$770	$770	$770	$770	$770	$770	$770	$770	$770	$770	$770	$770	$9,240
Membership dues	$372	$0	$0	$0	$0	$212	$0	$0	$536	$0	$0	$0	$1,120
Subscriptions	$0	$221	$0	$0	$0	$0	$221	$0	$0	$0	$0	$221	$663
Telephone	$6,997	$6,997	$6,997	$6,997	$6,997	$6,997	$6,997	$6,997	$6,997	$6,997	$6,997	$6,997	$83,964
TOTAL:	$102,167	$99,412	$99,064	$101,564	$98,972	$99,276	$104,912	$102,247	$102,689	$104,581	$102,191	$107,492	$1,224,567

XYZ Support Center Operating Plan

come from it. The best scenario is one in which you can quantify the benefit. In the support center, employee salaries and benefits represent between 70-80 percent of the entire budget. This means that almost any benefit you quantify will be tied back to reducing the need for future new hires in the support center. In an internal support center, you can also cite increased employee productivity and the cost savings that entails. For example, the justification for a new phone system needs to be in terms of increased productivity of your customers because they will wait less time to receive service and get back to work more quickly, and in reduced future headcount needs in the support center because the phone system will enable more efficient use of analysts' time.

At a new internal support center that I implemented, the entire first year's startup costs were justified in terms of the productivity gains realized by the employees not having to fix their own computers. The vast majority of the company's employees were highly compensated engineers who fancied themselves computer geeks as well. With the implementation of a support center, they were no longer expected to fix their own computers; the cost savings in terms of the employees' time were huge.

When speaking to executives in your company or organization, rest assured that they live, breathe and die by management of revenues, expenses and profits. Speak to them in this language and they will understand you; otherwise, you risk not being heard.

Strategic Plans

One of my joys as a support center executive was to create plans for what the support center would look like in two to three years. This exercise, which I did at the end of the fiscal year, took me out of reactive mode – the day-to-day fire-fighting – and into a strategic, proactive, future-oriented state of mind. What will our support center look like, feel like, be like in the future? What this visioning provided was a template for the center's future work, both short- and long-term. The result was a strategic plan for the next two years.

What are the elements of an effective strategic plan? Consider these as possibilities for your plan:

- **Market and competitive pressures and new products that will affect the support center.**

  The support center manager examines the market in which the center operates and predicts what trends and changes will affect service delivery. For example, if a competitor looks threatening, the plan will identify the threat and provide a plan to address it. New products, such as the introduction of the Windows Vista operating system, must be anticipated. These new releases will make demands on the support center that must be planned for.

- **Headcount requirements.**

  Given the new-product and competitive pressures that may raise headcount requirements, along with the proposed technology tools that may reduce headcount requirements, what will the net staffing level be in two to three years?

- **Staff development requirements**.

  New competitive pressures and new-product rollouts may require an upgrade in staff skill levels. Document the training and development that the staff will need in order to function optimally in the future.

- **Procedural changes.**

  Procedural changes could be needed to accommodate the anticipated service demands.

- **New service delivery models.**

  New support tools may make possible support delivery options that heretofore were impossible to conceive. Describe and plan for these new support models.

- **Customer satisfaction and loyalty.**
  What are the support center's goals for customer satisfaction and loyalty, and how will they be measured? The support manager must include plans to achieve these goals.
- **Support tools needed to sustain service levels.**
  This may include web chat, co-browsing, and self-healing and self-diagnosing technologies. What new support tools will be needed to provide these new support modalities?
- **Financial projections.**
  Given all the plans included in the document, what are the financial implications? I used to include budget projections for the next two years in my plans. I also included return on investment (ROI) calculations on proposed capital expenditures, if sufficient data were available. If not, I would calculate the ROI later, but before gaining approval for the purchase.

The benefits of writing a formal strategic plan were that I could clarify my vision for the future of the support center, then communicate it both up and down the organizational structure. I shared the strategic plan with both my manager and the entire support center, and explained exactly what it meant and what people might anticipate.

The manager of a small support center manager can do a brief version of the strategic plan by periodically conducting a SWOT analysis for the support center. SWOT stands for strengths, weaknesses, opportunities and threats. I use a diagram such as the one on page 13 to conduct a SWOT analysis.

The questions in each quadrant would help me think strategically about the current situation in my support center, what we do well and what we could do better, and future events, such as product introductions or market changes, that could be either opportunities

Strengths:
What do we do well?
What are our recent accomplishments?

Weaknesses:
What don't we do at all?
What do we do less well?

Opportunities:
What changes can we make to address future needs?
What ways can we better assist customers?
How can we build on our strengths?

Threats:
What could change our ability to go forward with plans?
What is holding us back?

SWOT Analysis

or threats to my group or the company.

The opportunity to think strategically is a luxury to most overworked support center managers. Each manager owes it to her group to take a few hours every quarter to review the strategic plan or SWOT analysis by making notes on progress made and what initiatives need more emphasis. The time you spend doing this is well worth it in terms of keeping the support center on progress and in thinking about future challenges.

Best Practices – Strategic Leadership

1. Create a mission statement that aligns with the corporate mission, purpose and/or objectives.

2. Create annual operational goals and objectives that align with the corporate goals. Cascade goals down to the analyst level, showing the relationship to the overall goals at every level.

3. Create financial reporting for the support center. If the support center is too small to warrant its own financials, the support manager should be aware of his budgetary decisions and be given some discretionary spending, such as for team-building and recognition.

4. Annually, create or revise a strategic plan or SWOT analysis for the support department that analyzes the market or internal conditions that the support center must operate within and the continuous improvement initiatives for the center. Review the plan quarterly.

## CHAPTER TWO

Setting Customer Expectations

WHETHER THE SUPPORT CENTER serves internal corporate customers or external ones, whether the support center has five analysts or 55, best practices dictate the need to set expectations with customers before they call for assistance. Every support center needs to create a friendly, readable document that tells customers what to expect from the support center and how to get it. If there is no definition of what to expect, each customer will have different service expectations and the center will never be successful in meeting or exceeding them. Managing expectations is an important activity for all support centers.

In internal support centers, the document that sets expectations for support delivery is called a service level agreement (SLA), and it is usually a negotiated agreement. External support centers call their document any number of things, such as a service level agreement or a support guide, but it is generally a description of the services that the customer chooses to pay for. Often, high-tech companies will offer customers several standard service options, such as premium or standard service, but the details of the offerings are standardized and sometimes not negotiable.

Service Level Agreements – Internal Support Centers

Service level agreements are contracts or agreements between the IT service groups and their customers. SLAs set expectations for conduct and performance for both parties in the agreement. SLAs generally establish the following:

- Response and resolution goals for handling incidents.
- Hours of operation.
- Service up-time goals.
- Support performance metrics.
- How support requests are handled both during business hours and after-hours, including escalation procedures.
- How quality is assured and measured.
- How to contact the support center.
- Reporting of SLA-related activities, such as the number of support requests resolved within targets.
- Prioritization of support requests.
- Scope of support, or what is supported and what is not.
- What the customer is expected to provide when seeking support, such as employee identification number, what product he is having trouble with and what he has already tried.

Service level agreements can be created in several ways. An overall SLA can be created between an IT organization and its customers; this is most common in small to medium-sized organizations and is the most straightforward method. Another approach is to create separate SLAs for customer groups that have vastly different requirements, such as the accounting department and the sales department. This works well when the different customer groups use different combinations of IT services (e.g.: the sales group uses Microsoft Office Suite and sales applications, whereas accounting uses Microsoft Office Suite and accounting applications). In large organizations, SLAs may be created for each IT service provided (e.g.: separate SLAs for the Microsoft Office Suite, accounting applications and sales applications). For this discussion, we will assume that one SLA covers all services and all customers, but the principles are the same for all approaches.

How to Create an SLA

The heart of an SLA is the response and resolution time promises you make to the customers. It is impossible to make any time commitments to customers unless all internal support groups, including the support center and all its escalation groups, have agreed to what they can deliver. Therefore, the best way to start creating an SLA is to negotiate what is commonly called an operating level agreement (OLA) with the internal IT groups. Once these groups can agree to what response and resolution times are feasible, only then can the IT organization approach the customers and negotiate the SLA. Please note that many IT organizations are not yet ready to promise resolution times; this is a metric to grow into as more discipline, better processes and better teamwork are developed among the IT support groups.

Before negotiating an SLA with customers, it is best to agree on feasible response and resolution times with other IT support groups. These commitments form the basis of an operating level agreement (OLA).

For many small organizations, an OLA can be simply an agreement about response and resolution times (see page 22 for a deeper discussion of response and resolution times).

In addition to OLAs, a support center must consider what ITIL calls underpinning contracts (UCs). UCs are agreements with outside, third-party vendors that provide support and services to your customers. An example of a UC is a contract with a vendor that provides printer and copier maintenance in your offices. You must ensure that the UCs and their response/resolution times align with and support the SLA promises.

Once an OLA is established, a draft of the SLA can be created. Many CIOs and IT directors like to create an IT advisory board that helps IT set strategic direction, prioritize competing IT projects and be the voice of the customer to IT management. The IT advisory board should have representation from each major department in the company or organization. IT management should present the SLA to and negotiate it with this group. All meetings should be recorded, either by a secretary or by audio recording, in order to retain the feedback gathered.

A service level agreement template is included in the reference CD for use with this book; see page 279 for purchase information.

Many internal support centers create a customer brochure that describes the highlights of the SLA, especially the elements that pertain to how a customer obtains support, such as how to contact the support center, hours of operation, how to access online services, etc. In this way, the support center converts the SLA into a marketing piece that can be used in many settings. We will discuss marketing ideas in Chapter Three: Marketing.

Support Guides – External Support Centers

In external support centers, the company generally requires a new customer to sign a lengthy legal contract that covers all aspects of the relationship. Contracts are written in language that users of the technology cannot understand, nor want to read. Many times, the end users of the product never even see the contract. Therefore, most external support centers create brochures for new customers and a page on the support web site that explain how to use technical support and what to expect when seeking support. Those "what to expect" documents contain many of the same elements included in a service level agreement, and in some instances, the technology provider may even name the document an SLA. The document may also be called the support guide, operations guide, customer guide or "How to Do Business With Us" guide. In this book, we will refer to it as the support guide.

A support guide should cover the following topics:

- What services are offered and the cost of each.
- How to contact the support center for assistance.
- Hours of operation.
- A description of how the support request will be handled when the customer contacts the support center.
- The escalation process.
- How the customer will be surveyed.
- How to access online support.
- What metrics the support center commits to (such as response and resolution times).
- Who to contact if the customer is not satisfied with support received.
- How many past versions of the product the support center will support. (Many software companies will only support the current version and the two previous versions of the software. It is costly to support old software versions. This stipulation must be accompanied with proactive communications to customers about impending deadlines to install new software.)

This information could be incorporated into a simple printed document, tri-fold brochure or glossy marketing piece, according to the importance of the customers. The support guide should be included in the customer's welcome kit that ships with the product. Many companies also post the document to the support web site so that customers can easily access it there. Many companies wish to set expectations with new employees at existing accounts. They might do this by conducting periodic newcomer webinars in which they present the information in the support guide and introduce how to do business with the support center. In addition, the support center might adopt a practice of emailing the brochure to each new employee who contacts the support center for the first time. These practices ensure that the support center continually sets expectations with new employees as they begin to use support services.

The external support center also needs to negotiate response and resolution goals with its escalation groups. Please refer to the discussion of operating level agreements on page 23. An OLA template is included on the companion CD that can be ordered from KR Consulting. Purchasing information is at the end of this book.

Priorities

In any support center, a best practice is to prioritize support requests according to the impact on the customer and the business. Priorities help the support center allocate resources appropriately, triage the issue and ensure that the customer gets a consistent level of service appropriate to the need. It is important to recognize that there are some requests that must be handled immediately while others can wait for resolution. There is a significant opportunity to satisfy customers if a support organization can fix an urgent problem in a timely manner. This makes it imperative to prioritize support requests, set response and resolution goals, and ensure that they are met. In order to maximize use of your support center and escalation groups' resources and keep your customers productive, problems should be prioritized according to impact and urgency. Impact defines how many people are affected and urgency describes how quickly it needs to be done. For example, a support request that affects only one worker must be prioritized lower than, say, a network outage or defect that affects a large number of customers.

Typically, a support center will define three to five priorities that correspond to the criticality of the support request. Priorities can be referred to by numbers or by words, such as critical, high, medium, low and planned. Many internal support centers keep a VIP (very important person) caller list composed of executives and important customers whose problems are automatically prioritized higher than normal. This practice recognizes the monetary impact created when these highly compensated people are not productive.

> **Typically, a support center will define three to five priorities.**

Assessing the priority of a support request is an important step in handling support requests. Support analysts should be trained to assess the priority of the support request as soon as they understand and record the full problem description. This step should be included in the process documentation for contact handling.

Here are several examples of priorities and their descriptions:

Priority Scheme 1 (Internal Support Center)

Priority level	Description	Examples/comments
1 Critical	An unplanned outage. A work stoppage. A VIP customer. An event that impacts revenues or corporate image.	Network outage. Email outage.
2 High	Any problem that prevents the user from carrying out her main operation and there is no acceptable workaround.	Unavailability of an accounting module.

Priority Scheme 1 (Internal Support Center) – continued

Priority level	Description	Examples/comments
3 Medium	Any problem affecting a significant part of user's operations. Problems that impede meeting a pending deadline.	Report writer is inoperable. Printer down.
4 Low	Any problem that must be addressed within 24 hours (from the ticket issue time) but does not involve deadlines or work stoppage.	How-to question.
5 Planned	Any problem that requires ordering a part, doing research or meeting a specified completion date. Installations/moves/adds/changes.	Usually used by internal support centers.

Priority Scheme 2 (External Support Center)

Priority level	Description	Examples/comments
1 Critical	Any support request that is creating a work stoppage for a customer. Mission-critical defects. Significant defects that affect X number of customers. Any support request that has no workaround.	Critical defects.
2 Normal	Any problem that prevents the user from carrying out his main operation, workaround available.	Printing reports to a specific printer.
3 Low	A routine support request that does not impact business operations; how-to questions.	How-to print reports.

Response and Resolution Time Targets

The most significant section of the SLA or the support guide is the promised response and resolution targets. A best practice is to set response and resolution targets by priority, and to set an overall percentage goal (e.g.: 95 percent of the incidents) for attainment of the targets. Another best practice is for the support center to retain ownership of the incident throughout its lifetime. This does not mean the support center will resolve all incidents but that it is responsible for reporting on the aging of incidents, ensuring the customer's satisfaction with escalated support requests, and handling status requests from customers regarding open tickets

As demonstrated on pages 21 and 22, a wise support center will hammer out agreements among its internal escalation groups as to how they will respond to incoming incidents and how quickly they can resolve most support requests. These agreements are typically called operating level agreements (OLAs). Similar to service level agreements, OLAs set expectations for how each group will work together. Both internal and external support centers need agreements with each of the groups to which they escalate support requests. These agreements ensure that a support center analyst can promise response times to escalated support requests with the confidence of knowing that the escalation groups will respond.

A best practice is to set response and resolution targets by priority.

Many support centers, both internal and external, operate well with a simple agreement with each of its escalation groups that defines the response and resolution times to each priority level of the support request or defect that is escalated. The following matrix describes expectations for level 3's response time and overall resolution time goals. This could be the extent of an OLA for a smaller organization.

The following is an example of a response and resolution guideline matrix:

Priorities With Response and Resolution Time – Example
Attainment Goal = 95 percent of SLA targets

Priority level	Description	Support center escalation guideline	Level 3 response time	Communication frequency to the customer	Resolution time goal
1 Critical	Mission critical, affects many users	Escalate after 15 minutes	15 minutes	Hourly	2 business hours
2 High	Limited scope, no workaround	Escalate after 1 hour	30 minutes	4 hours	8 business hours
3 Medium	1 user, workaround available	Escalate after 8 hours	4 hours	12 hours	24 business hours
4 Low	Non-urgent requests	Escalate after 24 hours	8 hours	24 hours	48 business hours
5 Planned	Moves/adds/changes	N/A	N/A	40 hours	10-day maximum

Performance Metrics

Another section of a service level agreement that concerns the support center directly is the performance metrics. Most of these metrics govern the way the support center operates. Here are several examples of a performance metrics section, with corresponding industry best standards. Please note that the first example assumes that the support center uses an ACD telephone system, the second does not.

Although metrics are discussed in depth in Chapter Nine: Metrics and Reporting, a few comments should be noted here. When providing telephone support, the presence of an ACD determines the metrics that you can measure. In the first example, service level (one method of measuring the response time to incoming phone calls) and abandon rate both come from the ACD reporting. The second example assumes the absence of an ACD and the presence of a dispatcher, and measures the support center's

Performance Metrics With ACD

Metric	Performance goal	Industry best practices (averages)	
		Internal support center	External support center
Telephone service level (Alternative metric = average speed of answer)	X% answered in Y seconds	85% within 30 seconds	85% within 2 minutes
Abandon rate	X% or better	5% or better	5% or better
Percent of electronic support requests responded to within 4 hours	X%	80%	80%
First contact resolution	X% of contacts resolved at initial call	60-80%	Variable, depending on the complexity of the support requests
Percentage resolved at first-level	X% of contacts resolved without escalation	80-90%	80%
Average handle time	X minutes	8 minutes	25 minutes
% of customers who are satisfied with the support center (top box score)	X% or better	80%	80%

Performance Metrics Without ACD

Metric	Performance goal	Industry best practices (averages)	
		Internal support center	External support center
Asynchronous response times to phone calls	X% within Y hours	85% within 2 hours	85% within 2 hours
Percent of electronic support requests responded to within 4 hours	X%	80%	80%
First contact resolution	X% of contacts resolved at initial call	60-80%	Variable, depending on the complexity of the support requests
Percentage resolved at first-level	X% of contacts resolved without escalation	80-90%	80%
Average handle time	X minutes	8 minutes	25 minutes
% of customers who are satisfied with support center (top box score)	X% or better	80%	80%

responsiveness to incoming calls that are set up for callback. A target for average handle time (the average time it takes to work a support request) is included in many SLAs for internal support centers because it is an efficiency measure. If a support center is taking relatively longer to solve support requests, it is working less efficiently, and the business does not want to pay for that. In an internal support center, the corporation is paying the support center to serve its employees. External support centers may decide that average handle time is not something their customers care about or is not something the support center wants its customers to know.

Support Contracts for External Support Centers

External support centers must charge their customers for support. No matter what level of support customers choose, it is important to set expectations with them regarding the services they are entitled to.

An external support center can charge for support services in several ways, including hourly billing, pay per contact, call-packs (a flat fee for up to X number of support requests) and annual support/maintenance fees. Recognizing that customers may have differing service needs, many companies offer customers several service options from which to choose. Typically, a company might offer premium, standard and basic levels of support to its customers. Some companies use precious metals terminology (platinum, gold and silver) to denote their service offerings, while others may use descriptive phrases such as basic, standard and enhanced.

Many companies offer customers several service options from which to choose.

The reasons for creating multiple options are to recognize that one size may not fit all and to optimize revenues for the company. Typically, larger or more important customers expect a higher level of service than do smaller ones, and most times they are willing to pay for it. If you offer only one level of support, you may wish to consider approaching your biggest customers to ask them what extra services they would like to see and be willing to pay for. In my consulting practice, I find that many smaller companies shy away from offering different support options, thinking that all customers should be given outstanding service. It is true that all customers deserve outstanding service, but perhaps not all companies need extra services that you can charge more for. There may be money left on the table if the support options available do not cater to the needs of the larger customers – or worse, you are providing premium services at no additional charge. Conversely, you may risk losing some smaller customers who do not want or cannot afford the standard support offering.

Here is an example of three levels of service a company might offer:

- **A premium (platinum) contract**

    This contract commands a higher price, perhaps 35 percent or more of list price depending on the spectrum of services provided. This should be a profitable venture for a software company. It is designed for larger customers who demand more services and a better response time. A platinum contract might include some or all of these services (this is not meant to be an exhaustive list):

    o *All services offered in the standard (gold) support contract.*

    o *A named account manager:* This support analyst is responsible for proactively and regularly contacting the client and coordinating all service delivery to this client.

    o *Extended hours for support.*

    o *Special reporting of support activity:* The account manager may provide monthly reports of services used and response times.

    o *Guaranteed response time:* Highest priority response time to all incoming support requests.

    o *Free training:* All training webinars at no cost, plus instructor-led training.

    o *Yearly health checks:* A short professional-services engagement.

    o *Quarterly calls from executives:* VIP clients love to receive special attention from their vendor's decision-makers.

    o *Inclusion in a client advisory council:* Premium clients could be invited to participate in an advisory council that meets quarterly via phone and perhaps yearly in person. This group would act as a sounding board for all products and services and could provide vital feedback to company executives.

- **A standard (gold) contract**

  This contract is designed for the majority of customers who desire a full set of support services. The price for a standard contract in the support industry is currently 18-20 percent of list price. The standard contract might include:

  o *Access to live support:* Customers are entitled to contact the support center via phone and/or electronic support. Support analysts will respond to their support requests within standard time frames.

  o *Access to web-based support:* Access to whatever features are offered on the support web site, including the knowledge base, frequently asked questions (FAQs), product and documentation downloads, and customer forums.

  o *Access to new updates and new releases of the product:* New releases of the products they own, on a periodic basis.

- **A basic (silver) contract**

  The basic contract is designed for the cost-conscious customer who is mostly self-sufficient. Because of the complications with this contract, most support centers do not actively market this option. However, it may be an option that the support center needs to maintain in order to retain some customers. The basic contract might include:

  o *Access to web-based support:* Access to whatever features are offered on the support web site, including the knowledge base, frequently asked questions (FAQs), product and documentation downloads, and customer forums.

  o *Access to new updates and new releases of the product:* New releases of the products they own, on a periodic basis.

  o *Access to live support on a pay-per-hour or pay-per-incident basis:* Unless the issue is a defect-related support request, the customer must pay for the interaction. Some companies charge a flat fee per incident; others charge according to the time spent supporting the customer.

This provision gets complicated when the customer and the support center do not agree on what a defect is. When the specifications do not please the customer, it can be difficult to explain to a customer that the product is working according to specifications.

Best Practices – Setting Customer Expectations

1. Negotiate internal operating level agreements (OLAs) with the support center's escalation groups before promising response and resolution goals to customers. Some small support centers create a simple OLA by agreeing on the negotiated response and resolution time goals by priorities with their internal escalation groups.
2. Create a service level agreement (SLA) that describes the services provided to customers. For external support centers, this may be the customer contract.
3. Create a marketing document or brochure that highlights the elements of the SLA that are important to the customers, such as how to contact support and hours of operation. External support centers often call this the support guide.
4. Ensure that the support guide or key elements of the SLA are available to customers. Reach out to new customers by proactively sending them a support guide or brochure.
5. Create a priority scheme for incoming support requests.
6. Create a matrix that shows response and resolution time by priorities.
7. For external support centers, create a variety of support contracts that cater to segments within the customer base.

## CHAPTER THREE

Marketing

EVERY SUPPORT CENTER needs to market the good job it does – it is
not sufficient to serve customers well if no one knows about it.
Publicizing accomplishments to customers and internal management is important for both internal and external support centers.
Any activity that increases the awareness of the support center and
encourages customers to use its services in the most efficient manner is beneficial marketing.

The Association of Support Professionals reports that high-tech
companies find that more than 50 percent of their revenues come
from support-related services.[2] External support centers in these
companies need to protect that revenue stream with constant marketing to the established customer base. In internal support centers,
the company needs you to market your services in order to keep
customers (employees) productive. It has been clearly established
that underground support (support that bypasses the support center) is costly to a company or organization, and marketing helps
remind customers that the support center is their single point of

[2] *Association of Support Professionals, Maintenance & Services Ratios / 2006,*
www.asponline.com (Membership may be needed to access the report.)

contact (SPOC) for all IT-related support requests.

The smaller support center can conduct a "marketing on a dime"

The smaller support center can conduct a "marketing on a dime" campaign. campaign. The best practices included here are no- or low-cost activities, with a rare exception, that will increase the support center's visibility without demanding big investments, except of time.

Please refer to Chapter Eight: Support Web Site for marketing ideas that encourage the use of self-service options offered through the Internet.

Marketing for Internal Support Centers

Internal support centers are marketing to internal customers, usually employees of the company or organization. Helping customers use services better or become more efficient in their use of technology is a productivity gain for the entire organization, making marketing a requirement. Here are some ideas to consider:

- **Post statistics on the support web site.**

  "What we've done for you recently" could be a great title for a section on the main IT web page that prominently displays support center performance statistics such as average speed of answer, first contact resolution rate, mean time to resolution and customer satisfaction results. Be sure to include an explanation of each metric that highlights what it means to the customer. For example, "A high first contact resolution rate means that you get your answer immediately, on the first call."

- **Set up a table at the entrance to the cafeteria.**

  Several times a year, set up a table at the entrance to the cafeteria during busy times and staff it with support center personnel. Display a poster with each analyst's picture and bio that displays a title of "Meet the Voice You've Heard on the Phone." Stock the table with tri-fold brochures that describe the support services (refer to Chapter Two: Setting Customer Expectations for a description of what to include in the brochure), a small gift (candy is fine, especially if it is a Hershey's Kiss to show the love) and any other information pieces that are timely. Set up a computer and monitor that continuously loop through a PowerPoint presentation on how to use the support web site. Post a sign that says "The Technology Doctor Is In – Free Advice" and offer on-the-spot technical advice for customers who stop by.

- **Conduct lunch-and-learns.**

Customers need to learn to use technology so that it works for them instead of being a frustration. Lunch-and-learn sessions are great ways to chunk educational opportunities into small bites (not bytes!) and present them during 45-minute presentations. This is also an opportunity for the analysts who present the classes to practice and improve their presentation skills. Publish the schedule of classes in as many places as possible.

- **Present technology fairs.**

This event needs to be coordinated with the entire IT staff. Many support centers present a yearly technology fair that highlights what the IT group is doing for customers, the new technologies that will be released and the services provided by the support center. The support center can set up a table similar to the cafeteria table previously described.

- **Have "The Technology Doctor Is In" sessions.**

This is for support centers that are co-located with their customers. If not, this involves travel to customers' sites (oops, that removes this idea from the low-cost category). Choose an area of the company – a floor perhaps or a department – and send a support analyst to visit customers at their desks to do proactive support activities. This effort prevents small problems from becoming big problems by fixing them early. Be sure to publicize this activity via posters, corporate newsletter articles and other vehicles. If your support center has suffered from a bad reputation in recent times, this is one of the quickest ways to turn around customers' perceptions. Who can resist an eager and earnest support analyst who proactively shows up to offer assistance?

- **Establish technology advisory councils.**

  In conjunction with other IT managers, select individual customers to join an advisory council. Good candidates for membership on the council are people who are informal leaders in their departments (not necessarily the top manager) and those who complain a lot about IT but have a proclivity for knowledge of IT issues (I call these people "good critics"). By including good critics on your council, you have an opportunity to turn them into your biggest advocates. Ask the council for advice on prioritizing upcoming technology projects, increasing user acceptance and implementing cost-cutting measures.

- **Distribute periodic newsletters from IT.**

  This e-newsletter might include technical tips and tricks from the support center, notice of new releases, a link to the forward schedule of changes (FSC), notice of known errors, etc.

- **Liberally distribute the support brochure.**

  Include the support brochure in all new-hire packets and/or have a support center representative conduct the IT training that every new hire in the company receives. Include the brochure with any new hardware deployment or upgrade so the customers are constantly reminded of the support center and how to receive support.

- **Leave thank-you cards after a desk-side support visit.**

  Create tent-cards, business cards or simple thank-you cards that a desk-side analyst can leave after each customer visit. The cards should include an expression of appreciation to the customer, how to contact the support center and perhaps hours of operation. Encourage the desk-side analyst to hand-write a note customized to the nature of the visit.

- **Report regularly to upper management.**
  Not all marketing is to customers. Many support centers suffer from a lack of understanding or appreciation from upper management. One way to market to executives is to send them monthly or periodic reports that include a description of the metrics included in the report and a brief commentary describing how the support center is reducing costs for the organization.

Marketing for External Support Centers

Although many of the above-mentioned marketing considerations apply to external support centers, a few major differences affect the means used. External support groups can influence a major revenue stream for the company, the maintenance and service fee. Many support centers are responsible for the customers' renewal rate of their annual maintenance/service fee. In addition, most customers of an external support center are remote, and face-to-face encounters are expensive.

With these major differences in mind, here are some activities to consider:

- **Formally remind customers of the services used.**
  Create a report for each customer that lists all support requests completed during the last year (or an appropriate time). Include the nature and severity of each request, its response and resolution time, and its current disposition (open or closed). Include also any customer satisfaction results gathered during that time. Send this report with a cover letter every six months or with the renewal notice for the annual support contract. This communication

demonstrates the value of the support center to the customer.

- **Post metrics to the support web site.**

  Just like an internal support center, the external support center should post its performance metrics in a prominent place on the support web site so customers can see what the support center has done for them recently. Be sure to include a narrative that details the metrics' benefits to the customer.

- **Create support center e-newsletters.**

  Often, the external support center will publish its own newsletter and send it periodically to customers. Include tips and tricks, features on upcoming releases, known defects, interviews with customers, "best customer" awards, recognition of most-frequent forum contributors, etc.

- **Present a support center booth or breakout session at customer conferences.**

  Customer conferences are great ways to meet face-to-face with customers who are otherwise remote. Exploit the event by presenting a support center booth or table on the tradeshow floor or in the meal room. Staff it with support analysts who provide on-the-spot technical support. Have computers at the booth to show customers the latest features or soon-to-be-released features. Give visitors some gift with the support center's contact information on it. Another best practice is to present a breakout session in which the support manager reviews the support center's recent achievements, then asks for feedback and recommendations for service improvements.

- **Report to upper management.**

  The support center should send monthly reports to upper management that show how the support center is increasing revenues and/or reducing costs through greater efficiency.

- **Consider site certification.**

  Warning: This is not a low-cost recommendation. Because of the costs involved, site certification seems best suited for mid- to large-sized external support centers that can use certification as a sales tool.

  Site certification is a way to market the support center's accomplishments both to customers and to internal executives. Site certification is an official "seal of approval" conferred by a third party that demonstrates the support center's adherence to best practices. Several certifications to consider are listed briefly here:

  o Service Capability & Performance (SCP) Support Standard program offered by Service Strategies Corporation. (I am an auditor for this program.) The program is focused on external support centers, although some internal support centers have participated in it. www.servicestrategies.com

  o Support Center Certification offered by HDI. This program is designed with the internal IT support center in mind, although some external support centers have participated in it. www.thinkhdi.com

Best Practices – Marketing

1. All support centers must market their services to at least two constituencies: internal management and customers.
2. No- to low-cost marketing opportunities abound and require only creativity and a sense of humor to find.
3. Post support center performance metrics on the support web site. Include a short description of why these metrics are important to the customer.
4. In all the reports sent to upper management, include explanations of metrics and what they mean to the company and to the customer.
5. Use company newsletters or e-newsletters from the support center to keep customers abreast of news from the support center and aware of technical tips and tricks to help them better use the products.

## CHAPTER FOUR

Support Request Handling Methods

ONE OF THE MOST BASIC ISSUES in providing support is the question of how to handle customers' support requests. Many times, a support center is created without a lot of thought given to this question – someone says, "Here's a phone extension, here are some desks, go find some people and let's start helping customers!" Sometime later, the support manager may wake up one morning and wonder how it all came about. Although it is better to intentionally plan your support request handling method at the start, all support centers have to examine this issue at some time.

The first question is whether or not to use the phone as the primary support medium. For all the internal support centers I have seen, the phone is uncontrovertibly the primary method of support. This is because the corporation or organization already has a PBX (a phone system that enables one main number and extensions off it) and the phone is the primary method of communicating within the company. For external support centers, the phone is not a given. Some external support centers, both large and small, offer only electronic or email support. The support analysts may use the phone for subsequent communications with the customer, but electronic means are used to initiate the support request. Of course, many external support centers offer phone support because the telephone is still the most common method of communicating in our society.

Beyond the basic decision of whether or not to use the phone lies several other options for designing the support request handling method. Due to the lack of resources, smaller centers use a wider variety of handling methods than larger centers. Read on to understand best practices in this complex area.

Common Support Request Handling Methods

In designing the support center's workflow, it is important to understand the different methods used to route or handle incoming support requests. With an understanding of the alternatives, a support center manager can choose the best one, or design a hybrid method that suits the needs of the business. Environmental variables that determine the best way to handle support requests include the complexity of the support requests; the availability of an automatic call distribution (ACD) system (a telephone function that directs the call to the next available analyst) or other advanced technologies; the need to entitle the caller before providing support; the average tenure of the support team; and the availability of a robust knowledge base and knowledge management process.

The support request handling process has two layers of design. The first question to ask is, "Will the support center provide real-time (also called synchronous) support or delayed (or asynchronous) support?" Real-time support connects the customer with an agent within the same interaction, whether it is via telephone or an Internet chat session. Real-time support uses some sort of technology to connect the customer to the analyst, whether it is a sophisticated ACD phone system, a tool that provides chat functionality or a simple "hunt group" on the phone system that rings the extensions of the support analysts in a pre-defined rotation or all at once. Real-time support requires that sufficient staff is available to answer incoming support requests, or the customer could hold indefinitely. Especially in smaller support centers, real-time support could require more analysts than delayed support because of the random arrival patterns of phone calls. Delayed support is commonly provided via email, electronic case entry or telephone callback and is characterized by a delay in time for a response from the support analyst to the customer.

The first question to ask is, "Will we provide real-time (synchronous) or delayed (asynchronous) support to our customers?"

A support manager may say it is the support center's intent to provide real-time support but may offer the customer the option to leave a voicemail if she does not wish to hold for the next available analyst. In this case, the support center switches from real-time to delayed support when the customer leaves a voicemail.

The real-time versus delayed response decision has to do with the initial handling of the interaction. Past that, any of the following methods can be provided in either a real-time or a delayed response. The following methods describe what happens after the initial step.

There are four major ways to handle incoming contacts. You may hear them called different names, but in this discussion they are referred to as:

1. Dispatch method
2. Expert groups method
3. Touch and hold method
4. Tiered method

These methods are not mutually exclusive; they can be combined to design the optimal support handling method for the unique needs of the support center. Additionally, each method has its advantages and disadvantages. Often, a support center will use one contact handling method early in its history, then evolve to another. The tiered support method is most common in support centers of all sizes, but some sophisticated support centers grow out of this approach, as we will see.

Dispatch Method – The Telephone Operator

Like the telephone operators of olden days, the dispatch method uses people to front-end the call and connect the caller to the correct party. The dispatch method uses employees who are not trained to troubleshoot a technical question to answer phones or direct an electronic support request. In a phone scenario, the dispatchers query the caller for demographic information such as name, customer number and problem type, which they enter into the service management system, then dispatch the record or transfer the caller to a trained support analyst. Dispatchers can use their knowledge of the analysts' specialties to direct the caller to the person best suited to handle that particular issue. The dispatchers generally distribute the calls based on their knowledge of each analyst's existing workload. This method is often referred to as the "human ACD."

The dispatchers generally distribute the calls based on their knowledge of each analyst's existing workload.

The dispatch method works best for more-complex support situations in which the analysts must conduct research to resolve most calls. It also is employed in situations in which the caller's entitlement to receive support must be validated, such as a software company that charges customers a maintenance fee that includes access to the support center. It does not work well when customers pose quick and easy questions, such as password reset requests or simple how-to questions about an application.

This method is used by most support centers in assigning electronic support requests to analysts, and it works well because electronic requests are an asynchronous (non-real-time) form of communicating. Generally, a supervisor or manager performs the duties of the dispatcher by watching the email queue throughout the day and assigning incoming support requests to people on their team. Alternatively, some support centers rotate the dispatcher duties of assigning electronic support requests among analysts by identifying a different dispatcher every day or half-day. See the electronic support requests scheduling considerations in Chapter Fourteen: Staffing and Scheduling.

The dispatch method can be used in both real-time and delayed scenarios, although it is more commonly deployed in delayed situations. To use the dispatch method in real time, the organization must staff sufficiently so that the customer's phone call or contact is answered in real time by both the dispatch group and by the analyst group. Some large technology companies employ the dispatch method to entitle the customer, set up the support request in the service management system and direct the customer to the right support organization. Because these companies provide support on many products and many configurations, their dispatchers are well trained to ask questions that determine which group to direct the customer.

> **Some large technology companies employ the dispatch method to entitle the customer, set up the call in the service management system and direct the customer to the right support organization.**

The following is a high-level diagram of the dispatch method.

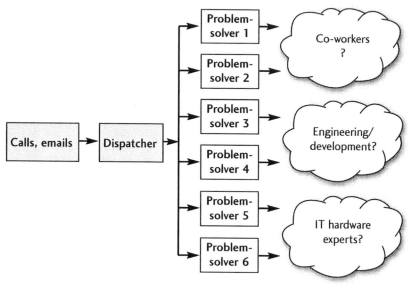

Dispatch Method

Advantages and Disadvantages of the Dispatch Method

The advantages include:

- The support center avoids the cost of implementing an automatic call distribution (ACD) phone system. This is a common reason that small centers use the dispatch method.
- It off-loads entitling the customer and setting up the support request in the service management system to lesser-paid members of the support center. For some support centers, entering in the customer's information and recording the nature of the support request can take several minutes. This task does not require a highly compensated support analyst's knowledge. This can represent a cost savings for the center.

- Customers speak to a human being every time they call in (unless all the dispatchers are busy and the caller is sent to voicemail). If they have to wait for the next available analyst, at least they have already spoken to someone at the company. Some companies prefer to provide the human touch and may actually increase the number of dispatchers in order to handle the volume.

Some disadvantages are:

- It may be more costly to staff the dispatcher queue with employees than to invest in an ACD phone system that does their job automatically.

- Customers may not always be directly connected to someone who can solve their problem, which creates a callback situation. Callbacks can be inefficient because customers are not always available when the analyst calls them back. It can also contribute to customer dissatisfaction with the service.

Without an ACD, the support center lacks the ability to track important metrics, such as abandon rate.

- Without an ACD, the support center lacks the ability to report and track several vital metrics, such as abandon rate, average speed of answer or service level, average handle time, and average talk time.

This method works best for:

- Support centers that provide complex support and have long average handle times (as a rule of thumb, long average handle times are defined as greater than 20 minutes). Especially if the support center is small (fewer than 10 analysts), providing real-time support may be more costly in terms of staffing than providing delayed or callback support.

Pitfalls to Avoid

In using the dispatch method, one practice that generally does not work is to put incoming support requests in a central queue and instruct analysts to work the queue in first-in, first-out order. In this scenario, it is human nature to select the most amiable customer to work with next, and "cherry-picking" of support requests is inevitable. It is much better to supply the dispatcher(s) with support analysts' schedules, areas of expertise and access to their workload to enable the dispatcher to assign support requests to a specific individual. Many support centers create specialized training for the dispatchers and give them detailed instructions on how to answer the calls (if using telephone support), how to set expectations for a callback time and how to assign support requests to analysts.

Another alternative is available to support centers whose service management system has a robust notification feature. If support requests go untouched for a period of time, the system can be programmed to send email, pager or BlackBerry notifications to increasingly higher levels of management, alerting them to the aging ticket. This method is best used in escalation situations rather than in initial contact with a support analyst.

Expert Groups Method – The Toll Booth

The second contact handling method is called expert groups, in which callers are directed to a small group of analysts who specialize in a certain area of technology. This method can be used in conjunction with the dispatch method or with an ACD system that distributes calls to the groups. Think of lines of cars waiting at a tollbooth or lines of shoppers waiting to check out in a grocery store. Both commonplace scenarios demonstrate the concept of expert groups, in which the customer joins a line, or queue, that represents a subset of the total number of customers waiting for service. Imagine selecting a line for a tollbooth only to realize that your tollbooth operator is highly inefficient and takes twice as long to make change. Your line inches along while the other lines seem to zip through their tollbooth. Or, at the grocery store, you get in a line that seems about the same length as the others, only to discover that the customer at the front of the line has 25 coupons to cash in, making your wait longer than it would have been in another line.

In technical support, an application of this method is to create analyst groups to handle PC, Unix and Macintosh calls, and each group is composed of experts in that platform. Sometimes support centers create expert groups along product lines or applications and direct customers according to the product group for which they have a question. Another application is to create groups to handle certain types of customers, such as platinum, gold and

Some expert groups could be PC, Unix or Macintosh support, or customer groups such as premium customers

silver customers; these designations are common in support centers that charge for support and have created different packages of services for customers.

Years ago, I managed a small support center of about 20 analysts at a software company. We created an expert group of four analysts to handle the company's premium customers' support requests because we wanted to provide them direct access to the best analysts in the company. What perplexed us was that these customers often had to wait longer than the other customers (even though the premium customers paid more for their support contract), so we continually added headcount to the premium group. However, when we added headcount, there were times when the premium group sat idle while the rest of the group was busy with calls. When

I learned about Erlang and the economies of scale in managing support queues, I changed the way we handled the premium customers. Using the ACD's dialed number identification feature, we gave premium customers highest priority in the queue so they were answered before other callers, but their calls were directed to the general pool of support analysts. We changed the premium analysts' job to an account management position, in which these senior analysts were responsible for proactively managing the premium customers' support requests and coordinating the many services these customers needed. By doing this, we reduced the headcount needed to provide premium service, ensured a high level of responsiveness to the high-value customers and maintained optimum utilization of my analysts' time.

This diagram shows how the expert groups method works.

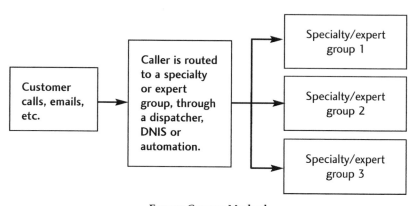

Expert Groups Method

Disadvantages to the Expert Groups Method

There is an important disadvantage to this method. Because there is a tendency to believe that you are serving customers better with specialized service, expert groups can be seductive. What you really are doing is providing premium level service to customers who may not be paying premium prices. The expert groups method is expensive to provide because it requires more people than a consolidated queue.

To illustrate the concept that expert groups require more people, we need to use Erlang calculations. Agner Erlang was a Danish mathematician who created a formula that accounts for the random arrival pattern of incoming support requests and calculates how many people are needed to staff a given queue. Inputs into Erlang calculations are:

- Average handle time (AHT).
- Number of support requests expected within a given time period.
- The response time to the incoming requests, usually expressed as a percentage of calls answered within X seconds (service level).

Erlang calculations were used to create the following illustrations. The first matrix shows how many analysts are needed to staff the expert groups mentioned above (PC, UNIX and Mac). For each group, we assume an average handle time of eight minutes and that 85 percent of calls are answered within 120 seconds. Each group, however, receives a different number of support requests within the hour interval of time. Note that the calculated occupancy percentage, which represents the amount of time during the hour that analysts are doing phone work, is different for each group.

Expert groups			
	PC queue	Unix queue	Mac queue	Totals
Contacts per 60-minute interval	50	25	15	90
AHT	8 minutes	8 minutes	8 minutes	8 minutes
% answered	85%	85%	85%	85%
Answer time	120 seconds	120 seconds	120 seconds	120 seconds
Occupancy	67.34%	61.73%	44.44%	N/A
Number of analysts needed	11	6	5	22

What happens to the number of analysts needed if those expert groups are combined into one queue? This could occur if we cross-train a group of analysts to handle all three areas of expertise. Look at this Erlang calculation of a consolidated queue:

Consolidated queue (PC, Unix & Mac together)	
Contacts/60 minute interval	90
AHT	8 minutes
% answered	85%
Answer time	120 seconds
Occupancy	74.07%
Number of analysts needed	18

The number of analysts needed drops dramatically, from 22 to 18, just by consolidating the queues. This demonstrates the drawback to expert groups – the method simply takes more analysts to handle the same number of support requests, and thus is costly and highly inefficient. It is based on the economies of scale provided by a larger queue of incoming requests.

There are several Erlang calculators that support managers can download from the web. Please visit www.krconsulting.com for an up-to-date list of web sites from which to download handy calculators. Play with the calculations to get a feel for how queuing theory works. Vary the inputs into the calculations and notice the effects. For example, use the average handle time, the service levels and the number of contacts from the first column. Then iteratively increase the average handle time in 1-minute increments and notice the effect on headcount. Or, increase the number of contacts per hour one by one, and note that the headcount increases in a "stair-step" manner – meaning, the same number of analysts can handle increasing numbers of calls to a point, and then another analyst is needed to uphold the service level/speed of answer. The following graphic assumes a service level target of 85 percent within 120 seconds and an average handle time of eight minutes.

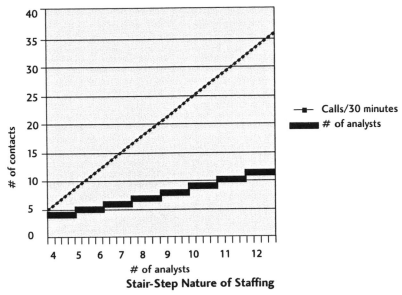

Stair-Step Nature of Staffing

Notice that in the graph, the number of contacts per half-hour climbs at a steady rate while the number of analysts climbs in a stair-step fashion. According to Erlang calculations, for example, five analysts can handle between eight to 10 calls per half hour and achieve the desired service level of 85 percent of calls answered within 120 seconds.

Advantages of the Expert Groups Method

The benefits to this system can override the need to save money. In environments in which customers pay for highly skilled and specialized service, it may be important to provide expert groups. Note also that in large support organizations that extend to hundreds of analysts, the expert groups method can be deployed without losing economies of scale. In an environment with a large number of analysts, the expert groups themselves are quite large. However, most small groups that use this method are unaware of its costly ramifications.

Pitfalls to Avoid

In general, smaller support centers should not consider employing the expert groups method, as it is inefficient for all but the largest support centers. Exceptions to this rule of thumb are support centers that can justify the inherent cost associated with a small queue by the relative amount of money or value the customers served represent to the company. Certainly, every support center will have analysts who develop deeper knowledge in certain areas than others, but it should be the goal of the smaller support center to ensure that all analysts are adequately trained and have access to a knowledge base in order to provide basic support on all supported products.

A good way to detect if your expert groups method is not working is to notice if one particular group is backed up with a large number of support requests while another group sits idle or is less busy. This is a clue that your analysts are not being consistently utilized, warranting an examination of your contact handling method.

Touch and Hold Method – The Bicyclist

In the touch and hold method, the support analyst who first handles the incoming support request is responsible for the support request until completion. This process does not include escalation, in the sense of passing the ownership of the support request to someone within the support center, except in the case of defects or other support requests that must be escalated to third-level groups. However, it does not preclude collaboration and seeking the counsel of informal experts within the support center. Subject matter experts (SMEs) will always develop naturally in any support center, depending on each individual's interests and talents. The individualized nature of this support request handling method is analogous to that of a competitive bicyclist – an athlete who performs on her own yet depends on a team of assistants to win.

In the book *The Art of Software Support*, authors Francoise Tourniaire and Richard Farrell[3] describe the use of a technical advisor within the support center to facilitate the touch and hold method. Technical advisors are available to the analysts to help them solve problems and find resources. I would warn that no analyst should be without resources to solve an issue, so the constant availability of the technical advisor is mandatory to make this method effective.

> **The individualized nature of this support request handling method is analogous to that of a competitive bicyclist.**

The touch and hold method is used in many support center contexts, although sometimes it is not a conscious decision. Many support centers, without understanding the options, start out with touch and hold by default. A new support center may have no choice but to default to this method, as it may not have any analysts who know more than others and can act as an escalation point within the center

The method assumes that each analyst is given adequate time to research issues that cannot be resolved during the initial contact with the customer. The support center needs a formal rotation schedule of on- and off-queue times (off-queue means that the analyst is not scheduled for any incoming queue, including phone, chat or electronic support request) for this method to work. Please refer to Chapter Fourteen: Staffing and Scheduling for information on creating an off-queue schedule.

This method works best with the availability of a robust

---

[3] *Francoise Tourniaire, Richard Farrell,* The Art of Software Support: Design & Operation of Support Centers and Help Desks *(Prentice Hall, New Jersey, 1998)*

knowledge base that allows analysts to find or enter solutions to approximately 80 percent of the support requests they encounter. If a knowledge base is not available or not adequately populated, this method will be less efficient than otherwise.

Advantages of the Touch and Hold Method

For support centers of any size that provide complex support, the touch and hold method works well. Touch and hold works best for support centers in which the analysts are highly technical and are accustomed to problem-solving independently. A support center that employs highly sophisticated network engineers or one in which analysts hold advanced degrees are good candidates for this method.

Disadvantages of the Touch and Hold Method

There are several situations in which the touch and hold method does not work as well as it does in a complex environment. One situation is when there is constant turnover in the support center and new hires to train. The touch and hold method works best with a stable workforce and well-trained, experienced analysts. The method may not provide enough structure for new hires looking for assistance when they are unsure of answers. It also does not work well in support centers where the speed of answer is an important performance metric. The tiered method works better in this case because it ensures that first-level analysts escalate the responsibility for a support request when they have exhausted either their knowledge or the time available. Escalation frees up the first-level analyst to take the next call or electronic support request, ensuring a quicker response time to customers.

Pitfalls to Avoid

No analyst enjoys coming to work to fail.[4] In support, that means

4 *Ray Marchand, RADAR Solutions Group*

that each analyst must know that there are resources to help her resolve questions that customers pose. Even in the touch and hold method, it is important to provide analysts access to employees with more experience or expertise and who have the time to help resolve the customer issues. Technical advisors should understand that their first responsibility is to be available to other analysts. Some companies augment the technical advisor by providing resources from development on an office-hours basis – the development employee posts weekly office hours, during which anyone in the support center can stop by to ask questions. This ensures that the support center has access to development's expertise.

> **Even in the touch and hold method, it is important to provide analysts access to employees with more experience or expertise.**

Knowledge management processes that capture the knowledge of experienced employees also help the touch and hold support method. See Chapter Six: Knowledge Management for a description of knowledge management processes.

Tiered Method – Hospital Emergency Room Triage

The fourth method is called tiered support, which refers to the process of escalations to or seeking counsel from increasingly more technical resources. It is similar to triage used in hospital emergency rooms, in that the manner in which the issue is treated depends on the urgency of the problem. The goals of tiered support are to direct urgent problems to employees who can solve them and to resolve approximately 80 percent of all support requests received before escalating to the next tier. The tiered method starts with self-service (phone-based IVR systems and web-based knowledge bases and FAQs) for many organizations today who consider self-service to be level 0 support:

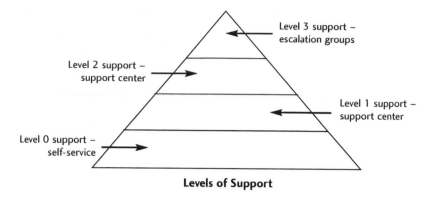

Level 3 support –
escalation groups

Level 2 support –
support center

Level 1 support –
support center

Level 0 support –
self-service

Levels of Support

Optimally, the goal is for 80 percent of the support requests to be resolved at each level, while 20 percent are escalated to the next level.

Typically, two tiers of this process reside in the support center. The first tier or level is composed of well-trained analysts who receive all incoming support requests (perhaps escalated from self-service). Level 1 analysts have access to level 2 analysts, who have deep technical and business knowledge, to help resolve the support request. Second-level, or senior, analysts are available to first-level analysts via telephone or via instant messaging, if it is available in the support center. Larger support centers create an internal ACD queue that the senior analysts log into in order to be accessible to first-level analysts via phone. It is a best practice to create a second instance of the database and log all calls placed by the frontline analysts to the senior analysts. Reports run on this data can help managers identify training opportunities for both individuals and teams.

> **Typically, two tiers of this process reside in the support center.**

Tiered support can be provided in real time using the phone or chat system, or can be used in a delayed support environment.

The tiered support method looks like this:

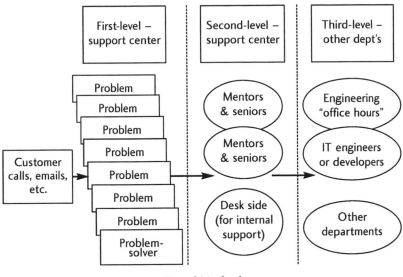

Tiered Method

Escalations

Inherent in the tiered support model are escalations.

A well-conceived and well-executed problem escalation process is as essential to the support center's effectiveness as is the triage process in a hospital emergency room. Fortunately, we do not often deal with life-or-death situations. However, a network outage or a bug that brings down a mission-critical application is a serious and costly event for a company. We need to be ready with an escalation plan that involves a parade of the proper professionals to solve problems quickly and efficiently.

Escalation can sometimes connote the transfer of an angry customer to a supervisor or manager for further handling (hierarchical escalation), but in this discussion we will use the term escalation to mean escalating a support request to an analyst with more expertise (functional escalation).

Planning the Process

Escalations start with a service level agreement (SLA) that defines the severity rules used in prioritizing incoming support requests. We have already examined response and resolution times promised according to severity in Chapter Two: Setting Customer Expectations in the section on service level agreements. Many support centers have these response and resolution target times built into their service management system, so the targets are automatically displayed in the case record.

It is the support center's responsibility to set the severity level of the support request at the time of service delivery, and in many instances it is not a negotiable issue with a customer. However, some support centers allow the customer to set a priority level in addition to the by-the-book severity level. In this way, a severity 3 (normal) problem can be tempered with a customer-set priority 1 rating, perhaps because the customer is unable to run a report needed to meet a deadline. The support center can consider the customer-set priority rating as the ticket is worked. This can become complex, as centers set up a matrix like this to manage the priorities/severities:

It is the support center's responsibility to set the severity level of the support request at the time of service delivery.

	Severity 1	Severity 2	Severity 3	Severity 4
Priority 1	Impact 1	Impact 1	Impact 2	Impact 3
Priority 2	Impact 1	Impact 2	Impact 3	Impact 4
Priority 3	Impact 1	Impact 2	Impact 3	Impact 4
Priority 4	Impact 1	Impact 2	Impact 3	Impact 4

The impact of the issue is what determines the actions of the support center and its support partners. Further discussion on this subject assumes only one severity designation, not the intersection of severity and priority.

Severity 1 (critical) requests are usually escalated immediately to a third-level group after the support center gathers a thorough problem description. For non-critical severities, the frontline analyst first attempts to resolve the issue. If the frontline is not able to solve the problem, the ticket is escalated (typically in real time) to a second-level analyst within the support center.

First-Level Support

For escalations to work well, first-level support analysts need three things:

1. Training, both initial and ongoing.
2. Access to a knowledge base.
3. Access to senior analysts within the support center who can help them resolve issues.

Each of these elements will be covered in this chapter. Support centers that wish to strengthen their support request resolution process must develop these three supporting elements.

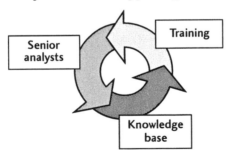

Three Elements Needed for Optimal Escalation Management

Second-Level Support

Senior analysts within the support center often provide second-level support. To be fully effective, the senior analysts must be available for questions from the frontline on a real-time basis. In larger support centers, seniors actually staff an internal ACD queue or are immediately available via instant messaging (IM) to assist the support analysts on the phones. In small centers, they can be available by IM or in a more informal manner.

There are three ways that a senior analyst can help the frontline:

DESCRIPTION	WHEN TO USE	BENEFITS	DISADVANTAGES
1. Frontline analyst puts the caller on hold and calls or IMs the senior to ask questions and get assistance.	When call volumes are low to moderate and the support request is not complex.	Immediate assistance; the frontline analyst learns by getting answers from the senior analyst.	None, except the annoyance of hold time to the customer.
2. After being contacted by the frontline analyst, the senior can conference in the call, making it a three-way call.	When the support request is complex or the frontline rep is unfamiliar with the support request.	Eliminates the "middle man" in the conversation; the frontline analyst learns by listening to senior analyst.	None, except the annoyance of hold time to the customer.
3. After being contacted by the frontline analyst, the senior assumes responsibility for the call, releasing the original analyst to take another inbound call.	As a last resort when call volumes are high and the problem is beyond the expertise of the frontline analyst.	Releases the frontline analyst to serve another customer.	Unless the senior methodically teaches the frontline, the frontline analyst does not learn how to solve that problem.

If the frontline analysts are providing web-chat support, the same procedure is used. However, email or electronic support does not demand such real-time assistance, so less formal ways of obtaining assistance can be used. (Please note, however, that customers now expect a quicker turn-around to their email inquiries than in the past. Therefore, many companies are embracing a four-hour response time goal to all email requests.)

The senior analyst either works the problem or recognizes that it must be escalated to third-level.

Third-Level Support

If second-level support in the support center is not able to solve a problem, the support request is escalated to third-level support groups, which are usually other IT or product development groups in the company. The challenge here is that the support request is now out of the support center's hands. The timely resolution of support requests escalated to third-level requires teamwork and accountability across organizational lines.

A best practice in support center management is to retain ownership of all tickets even after they have been escalated to other groups in the company. In ITIL terms, the support center is the single point of contact (SPOC) for customers. The reason for this practice goes back to customer behavior. Who did the customer first talk to about this problem? The support center. Who will receive a call from the customer if a status is needed on the problem? Again, the support center. Assuming "cradle-to-grave" ownership of all escalated support requests does not mean that support analysts must be the only ones to communicate with the customer. It is usually most efficient if the third-level analyst contacts the customer directly; however, some organizations find that if the third-level person contacts the customer, the customer is then more likely to contact that analyst or developer in the future instead of contacting the support center. (For this reason, some

> **A best practice in support center management is to retain ownership of all tickets.**

organizations do not publish the extensions of their developers.) Whatever communication guideline is used, support center management should monitor the resolution process and report resolution times plus SLA compliance to upper management. It also means that the support center contacts the customer, either via automated email or by phone call, when the escalated support request is closed. This not only creates a "warm fuzzy" feeling for the customer, but also ensures that support requests are resolved to the customer's satisfaction and – importantly – adds to the credibility of the support center.

The support center runs, from its service management system, both aging reports and service level agreement compliance reports. Aging reports summarize, for each escalation group, how many tickets are open and for how long they have been open. SLA/OLA compliance reports display each escalated problem, its severity, the elapsed time before third-level response, the elapsed time before resolution, and if that resolution was in compliance with SLA guidelines. The support requests that are escalated within the support center should be included in these reports as well. Refer to Chapter Nine: Metrics and Reporting, for examples of these reports.

These reports will be less effective if there is no one in the company who will enforce SLA/OLA compliance.

Word of warning: These reports will be less effective if there is no one in the company who will enforce SLA/OLA compliance. You must find an executive (the CIO, the VP of technology or the VP of development) who will make all third-level escalation groups accountable to their SLA commitments. Ideally, the reports that you generate are reviewed on a weekly basis so that the backlog of open tickets can be managed continually. Open-ticket reviews are usually conducted at the weekly staff meeting of the previously mentioned executive, in which all participating groups are represented. I've heard this meeting called the "rank and spank" meeting, in the sense that reviewing the aging report is the ranking and using public scrutiny on those groups that aren't closing tickets according to SLA guidelines represents the spanking.

The best escalation plans identify a problem coordinator who gathers a team of IT or product development analysts, as needed, to resolve an issue. The problem coordinator is assigned according to the nature of the problem. Often that person has the authority to pull colleagues off other projects in order to resolve a critical issue.

Follow-up and Closure

After an escalated support request is resolved, it is up to the support center to follow up with customers to ensure their satisfaction. As mentioned before, this puts the support center in the driver's seat, encourages customers to call again and gives customers the assurance that the support center is on top of things. The follow-up need not always be a phone call; sometimes a friendly email will do just fine.

Many support centers accomplish this step by creating a "resolved but not closed" status in their service management system. The third-level analyst enters this status code when the support request is resolved. The system then routes the ticket back to the support center, preferably to the analyst who originally took the call, for follow-up. If you do not have the staffing to do follow-up calls, you can configure your service management system to automatically send an email, but why pass on an opportunity to build customer loyalty? Most centers have periods during the week when call volumes are low and can schedule out-bound calls. Tickets are closed after the support center has successfully made contact with the customers and ensured their satisfaction. The support center may implement guidelines on how many times the analysts contact customers before the support request is automatically closed.

Some support centers conduct a weekly meeting that includes analysts of both the support center and escalation groups. The meeting's purpose is to review escalated tickets and discuss their resolutions. This is an educational opportunity for the support department that also becomes a forum for problem management in which all participants discuss the root cause of the support requests and plan actions to address them. Output from this meeting may go to the change manager for consideration.

When I managed a large technical support center for a financial institution, the group had poor efficiency metrics due the lack of a defined escalation path or tiers of support. Turnover was an issue in the group, as analysts did not see a career path for themselves. We created positions of senior analysts and defined an escalation process, similar to what is described here. The number of resolutions in the support center increased, the time to resolution decreased and retention of analysts improved. The development group that we worked with was especially happy because escalations to that group decreased after this process change.

Advantages of Tiered Support

The tiered method for contact handling is common in support centers because it efficiently handles most issues and provides a quick way to get access to more experienced analysts. It can be implemented with an ACD (automatic call distributor) telephone system or with simple hunt group functionality, in which all support center analysts' phones ring at the same time or may roll to other groups after a number of rings.

Tiered support directly addresses the inefficiencies that the expert groups method poses.

Tiered support directly addresses the inefficiencies that the expert groups method poses by directing incoming support requests to a large group of first-level analysts. Tiered support also offers career paths within the support center. As analysts gain proficiency, they can be promoted to the position of a senior analyst who provides second-level support.

For support centers dedicated to providing real-time support, tiered support is often the best way to free up frontline analysts to handle more incoming support requests. In these centers, managers set a guideline for the duration of a frontline call, after which the analyst is encouraged to escalate to second-level so they can take the next incoming call.

Disadvantages of Tiered Support

It is important to understand the drawbacks of tiered support. Tiered support does not give sophisticated customers access to expert analysts at first, although an effective escalation process should ensure that the process is efficient. If the support center delivers complex support to demanding customers that pay high support fees, expert groups with a tiered system within the expert groups or a touch and hold approach may work better. Tiered support does not offer the customer access to the same analyst for each support interaction. Some support centers with sophisticated phone systems allow customers to enter an open ticket or case number as they call; this information is used by the system to route the phone call to the analyst who last touched the case. If that analyst is not available, either the call is routed to a team member or the customer is offered the ability to leave a message for the analyst. Because the customer gets the next available analyst when calling the support center, support centers that provide premium service to some customers typically offer an account management service to complement the regular phone support and offer "one face to kiss" for the customer.

Pitfalls to Avoid

Often, escalating a call from first-level to second-level within the support center is done in real time: the senior analyst takes over a call while it is in progress. However, if the support request is escalated to either second- or third-level and the customer must wait for a callback, there is the potential for developing a backlog that must be managed. As in the expert groups, it is important that someone assign responsibility for escalated calls. Any queue of unassigned support requests has a tendency to languish or be cherry-picked by otherwise responsible employees, even if they are instructed to watch the queue and work the support requests in the order in which they arrive. Often the manager of the escalation group is responsible for assigning escalated support requests to appropriate personnel; the manager can distribute the workload equitably and manage around employees' vacations and sick times.

Email Support Versus Electronic Entry

Email support, in which customers send free-form emails to a support in-box, has inherent drawbacks. Because an email is not structured, a support center will often receive information from the customer that is insufficient to begin troubleshooting. There is nothing to stop the customer from sending an email that says only, "My computer won't work, please fix it." What ensues is an inefficient game of "tag," in which the support analyst either calls or emails the customer to clarify the request. If the customer is not available, the analyst must leave a message and wait for the customer to call back. This game can go on for days, consuming both the customer's and the analyst's time before the nature of the issue is established and resolution efforts can begin.

Several industry studies confirm the inefficiency of email support.

Several industry studies confirm the inefficiency of email support and show that email support is actually more expensive than phone support. This is due to the inefficiency described on page 66.

Unless the support center has an email management system that automatically logs incoming emails, there are additional disadvantages in providing email support, including:

- **Deleted or lost:** Emails that are directed to a central email box can be deleted and lost before they are properly handled, leaving the customer in the lurch.

- **Lack of metrics:** It is difficult to measure response times to incoming emails when they arrive in an email in-box. Without an email management system, there is no integration between the email function and the service management system, so recording the email's "Sent" time and response time is a manual process.

- **No auto-acknowledgement:** Unlike web-based entry forms, the customer does not receive an automatically generated acknowledgement of the email request that includes both the support request record number and the expected time of response.

It is much better to create a web-based entry form that requires the customer to provide data such as the platform, product, version and problem description. Some forms even request the customer to enter the request's priority level. The information is used to automatically create a record in the service management system. All reputable commercially available service management systems have a web-based case/ticket entry function that can be integrated into a company's Intranet or web site.

The benefits of web-entry are that the support request is automatically set up in the system, it already has much of the needed information in it, and an analyst can start working it immediately. In addition, an auto-acknowledge is sent to the customer and all the normal response-time metrics can be measured and tracked through the system. The time savings realized with this feature often convince support centers to phase-out all email support. This is best done over a lengthy period of time that allows the support center to prepare customers for the change. Marketing efforts might include a newsletter article announcing the availability of the web-based entry form and the date when the email box will be closed. The same information might be included in each support analyst's email signature section. Acknowledgements of emailed support requests could include this information also. As in any marketing campaign, the benefits to the customer should be highlighted repeatedly.

Choosing the Right Model

These four models are not mutually exclusive. You may use a hybrid, or combination, of two or more of the models. Some support centers use the dispatch method to assign support requests to expert groups and have tiers within the expert groups. It is important that you understand which method you use and why. Some good times to assess your support request handling method and ensure that it is serving you well include:

- When you implement a new service-management system.
- When you roll out new services to customers.
- When you release a major update of a product.

The following matrix can help you choose the right model.

	Dispatch	Expert groups	Touch and hold	Tiered (real time)
Size	Any size	Large centers	Large centers	Any
Real-time or delayed	Delayed	Either	Either	Real time
Availability of ACD	Yes or no	Yes or no	Yes or no	Yes
Complexity of support requests	More-complex support requests	More complex	Complex	Less complex; shrink-wrapped software support; internal help desks
Source of support request	Email, electronic	Any	Any	Telephone, chat
Analyst profile	Less experienced to well trained	Experts	Well trained and experienced	Less experienced analysts
Customer profile	Willing to wait for response	High value customers	Any	Any

Comparison of the Four Models

Best Practices – Support Request Handling Methods

1. Decide on the best handling method after considering the unique characteristics of your support center. Elements to include in your decision are size, complexity of support, availability of a telephone system, etc.

2. Define and document escalation paths for all support requests. Ensure that no analyst is left without resources to assist in resolving an issue.

3. The support center is the single point of contact for all support requests.

4. The support center retains responsibility for all support requests until they are completed. For escalated support requests, this means the support center runs response and resolution times reports and aging reports on open tickets and presents them to upper management so that escalation groups can be held accountable.

5. The support center ensures that all escalated support requests are resolved to the satisfaction of the customer. This can be done with a follow-up call or email to the customer.

## CHAPTER FIVE

Support Request Handling Processes

AFTER CHOOSING THE RIGHT SUPPORT request handling method for your support center, there are several steps needed to ensure that the method is fully documented, communicated to the analysts and supported by your service management system. In this chapter, we explore creating flowcharts and documentation of your process, processes to ensure timely escalations, and methods to categorize and manage support requests throughout their life cycle.

Documenting Your Support Request Process

Whatever method you use, it is important to document your process. A flowchart of the contact method process is a good way to initiate the process documentation and helps you see where inefficiencies exist. A flowchart also helps you visualize many of the functions that you will need to set up in the service management system, such as status values, escalations and notifications.

When creating a flowchart of your support request method, it is helpful to keep in mind the recommendation from Information Technology Infrastructure Library (ITIL) that cites the main incident handling activities as:

- Incident detection and recording
- Classification and initial support
- Investigation and diagnosis
- Resolution and recovery
- Incident closure
- Ownership, monitoring, tracking and communications

In addition, keep in mind that your flowcharts should cover, at the least, the following scenarios:

- The first-level analyst is able to resolve the support request on initial contact, whether he seeks assistance from second-level during the contact or not (first contact resolution).
- The first- or second-level analyst is able to resolve the support request, but only after researching the issue and re-contacting the customer (first-level resolution).
- At any tier in the system, the analyst cannot resolve the support request until the customer provides some information.
- The first-level analyst is unable to resolve the support request and escalates it to second-level resources (either a senior analyst or a desk-side support analyst). The second-level analyst closes the case.
- The second-level analyst is unable to solve the support request and escalates it to third-level. Third-level resolves the support request, or it is kept pending until a new release or patch is installed.
- The support request is a priority 1 and is escalated directly to third-level from the first-level analyst. Third-level resolves the support request.
- An electronic support request arrives in queue and must be assigned to a first-level analyst.

A flowchart of your process may look something like this (see next page). This flowchart and others that it references are available on a CD that complements this book. It is available online at www.krconsulting.com.

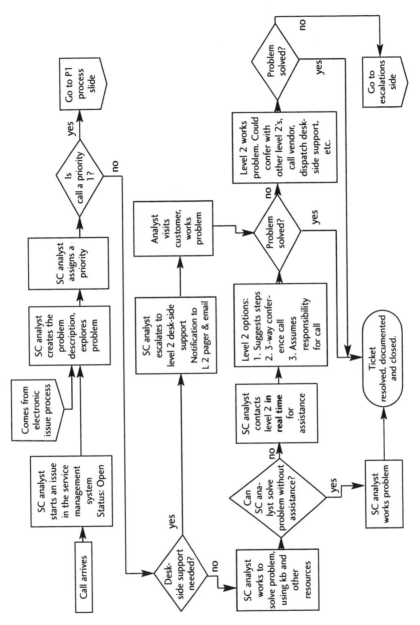

Support Request Handling Process

ITIL Considerations for Smaller Support Centers

ITIL differentiates between incident management, the goal of which is to restore service to the customer as quickly as possible, and problem management, which is concerned with identifying the root cause of incidents. In mid-sized to larger support centers, these two processes are assigned to different groups, where perhaps a third-level escalation group outside of the support center is tasked with problem management. Indeed, ITIL literature states that there is an inherent conflict between the goals of incident and problem management.[5] However, in small organizations there is no choice except to perform both incident and problem management in the support center. Problem management can be assigned to the senior analysts in the support center, who are sufficiently skilled and experienced to be able to research the root cause of the incidents they observe in the support center.

In small organizations there is no choice except to perform both incident and problem management in the support center.

Process Documentation

In addition to creating workflow diagrams, it is important to document your processes in writing. There are many reasons to do this, even if the support center is small:

- Unless a process is documented, each analyst will do it differently. Process consistency is a building block of good customer service. Customers do not want to get different treatment depending on whom they talk to in the support center.
- Documenting the steps to a process should force the support center to examine many possible ways to do it and decide on the best method. The act of writing the procedure then becomes a quality improvement exercise.
- Process documentation becomes the first entry into a knowledge base for the support center.

[5] *Stationery Office Books,* Introduction to ITIL *(Reading, UK: Stationery Office, 2005)*

• Process documentation becomes material for new hire training and eases the new hire's transition into the support center.

There is a reason that all of the quality programs – such as ISO, Six Sigma, the Service Capability & Performance (SCP) Support Standard certification program and HDI's Support Center Certification (SCC) program – all demand that processes are thoroughly documented. Unfortunately, the smaller support center cannot wiggle out of this mandate.

Larger support centers establish teams of people who are dedicated to researching best practices in processes, designing the center's processes, documenting them and training the analysts. That is not needed in a smaller center, but a yearly review of processes by a small group of analysts and the manager will ensure that the documentation is current and represents the best process for the support center.

In Appendix C, you can find a procedure template and example. You may wish to use this or a similar template for all your written procedures.

Logging All Support Requests

A best practice is to log all support requests that arrive in the support center. The benefit is a complete record of all work done in the support center, enabling you to accurately predict staffing levels and conduct root cause analysis. While some analysts may object to this guideline, many understand the benefits in terms of being able to view a complete history of the customer's contacts to support. In addition, logging all support requests, including wrong numbers and requests for assistance on unsupported products, fully documents the nature of the workload and the time spent.

A best practice is to log all support requests.

In order to encourage analysts to enter all phone calls, the support center should consider creating "quick calls" in the service management system. Quick call records are for wrong numbers, transferred calls and other short, repetitive calls that do not require a lot of detailed documentation, such as password reset requests. Quick calls should be structured so that no more than three mouse clicks are needed to record the incident. It may not be necessary to record the name of the customer for some quick calls. Most service management systems allow you to implement these types of records, and the payoff is enormous.

Adherence to the 100 percent logging mandate is tracked by comparing the number of incoming phone calls with the number of support requests logged in the service management system. This reporting assumes a record is kept of customers who call back on previously opened support requests. Many service management systems enable this by allowing the analysts to enter an activity sub-record in the case or a ticket that is counted as a new record for this purpose.

Status Fields

Status fields are important because they create triggers for notification and escalation. Because they are so foundational to your operation's success, it is important to give thought to creating them.

Let us go back to the seven scenarios that needed to be included in your workflow documents and see what status fields are needed to track the current state of a support request. At right is a sample of a completed status field worksheet.

You may wish to create a similar matrix that outlines the status fields that you wish to include. Notating the status field changes on the support request flowchart can also help you identify the correct status fields and when they change.

Notifications

Notifications are defined as communications or reminders that are sent to customers, analysts or other employees. They assist the

Status Field Worksheet – Example

Support request handling scenario	Associated status fields
1. The first-level analyst is able to resolve the support request on initial contact, whether she seeks assistance from second-level during the contact or not (first contact resolution).	Open Closed
2. The first-level analyst is able to resolve the support request, but only after researching the support request and re-contacting the customer (first-level resolution),	Open Work in process (WIP) Closed
3. At any tier in the system, the analyst cannot resolve the support request until the customer provides some information.	Open Pending – customer Closed
4. The first-level analyst is unable to resolve the support request and escalates it to second-level resources (either a senior analyst or a desk-side support analyst). The second-level analyst closes the case. First-level confirms resolution with the customer and closes the support request.	Open Assigned WIP Resolved Closed
5. The second-level analyst is unable to solve a support request and escalates it to third-level. Third-level resolves the support request, or it is kept pending until a new release or patch is installed. First-level confirms resolution and closes support request.	Open Assigned WIP Pending – update Resolved Closed
6. The support request is a priority 1 and is escalated directly to third-level from the first-level analyst. Third-level resolves the support request. First-level confirms resolution and closes the support request.	Open Assigned WIP Resolved Closed
7. An electronic support request arrives in queue and must be assigned to a first-level analyst.	Open Assigned

support center and its escalation groups to communicate support request status, to provide timely service and to meet SLA goals. Notifications can be sent via email, pager or wireless media. The service management system can perform time-based or automatic notifications/escalations.

When first implementing a service management system, most support centers create too many notifications. When customers or internal employees complain about the amount of email they get, the support center turns off several notifications. For example, sending notification to customers every time a support request is created for them (even if they telephoned the support center) is generally too much. Notification of an electronically created support request is sufficient.

The notification process that you create should be presented to all affected parties and negotiated. This is best done in the presence of the manager or director to whom all escalation groups report. This executive should be the ultimate arbiter of who is notified within the organization and when.

Be careful to limit the number of notifications sent to upper management. It is generally easier to set up notifications as you start out than to add them later, and it is usually a simple matter to turn off notifications. Given that, a good approach to notifications is to plan for all notifications that you can think of and then eliminate them as needed. There is one exception to this recommendation, which is to be careful to limit the number of notifications sent to upper management. These notifications should be reserved for emergencies or for breaches of SLA targets for priority 1 support requests

The following is a list of situations to consider as notification triggers:

- Notify the appropriate managers if a support request is not resolved within SLA guidelines.

- Notify the customer upon a status change to her support request.
- Notify the support center if a customer fixes or closes the problem independently.
- Notify assignee if there has been no edit on a ticket for a given time ("no touch").
- Notify analyst if customer requests a "callback."
- Notify customers automatically if production is down.
- Notify the manager if an employee creates a ticket (for internal support centers).
- Notify the manager if a project request for her area is entered.
- Notify the appropriate manager if a support request is not assigned within 10 minutes (i.e.: electronic requests).
- Notify the appropriate manager if a support request is pending for too long.
- Notify the appropriate manager if a request requires an approval (as in a new hire set-up request or moves/adds/changes in an internal support center).

To help you define a complete set of notifications, start with the support request handling flowchart. With its visual representation of the workflow, it offers reminders for notification opportunities. The SLA response and resolution matrix is another good vehicle for identifying notification opportunities.

The matrix for notifications regarding response and resolution time commitments on page 80 is a helpful guide to setting up SLA notifications.

Categorization of Support Requests

Categories are the basic building blocks of a support center's service management tool. They affect many support activities including reporting, escalations, priority assignments, knowledge management and knowledge searches. Categories provide the classification scheme for the support requests that you record and are keys

Escalated Issue Notification Process – Example

Priority	SLA response time	Initial, no-touch notification after escalation	After-hours notification	SLA response time	Open ticket notification after escalation	Risk of breach
1	15 min.	After 15 mins, to senior analyst. After 45 mins, to manager. After 60 mins, to backup manager.	After 30 mins, to senior analyst. After 60 mins, to manager. After 90 mins, to backup manager.	2 business hrs	Communication of progress every 30 mins until ETA is known, then hourly to customer, support center and other affected parties.	15 mins prior to breach of SLA response or resolution target.
2	30 min.	After 1 hour, to senior analyst. After 2 hrs, to manager. After 3 hrs, to backup manager.	After 2 hrs, to senior analyst. After 3 hrs, to manager. After 4 hrs, to backup manager.	8 business hrs	After 4 hrs, to senior analyst. After 5 hrs, to manager.	15 mins prior to breach of SLA response or resolution target.
3	4 hrs.	After 4 hrs, to senior analyst. After 6 hrs, to manager. After 7 hrs, to backup manager.	8:00 next business day, to senior analyst. 10:00 next business day, to manager. 11:00 next business day, to backup manager.	24 business hrs	After 24 hrs, to senior analyst. After 36 hrs, to manager.	30 mins prior to breach of SLA response or resolution target.
4	8 hrs.	After 8 hrs, to senior analyst.	N/A	Variable	Will show up on weekly reports.	60 mins prior to breach of SLA response or resolution target.
5	N/A	After 5 days, to manager.	N/A	10-day maximum		N/A

to retrieving and acting on the information in the support requests record. Because of the primal importance of categories, it is important to spend time creating a sound category scheme.

Categories provide the classification scheme for support requests.

Without careful thought and constant maintenance, category schemes can devolve into a tangled mess of duplicate, unused or overused problem types. This creates a situation in which the categories used to classify support requests in the support center become meaningless. As Jennifer Streitwieser notes in her article, "Designing Categories for Business Benefit,"[6] categories are a visible sign of the support center's effectiveness, as an unorganized category scheme reflects poorly on the support center. In addition, poorly designed schemes frustrate and de-motivate support analysts who use them.

Benefits of a good category tree are to:
- Organize groupings of support requests in reporting.
- Enable escalation of problems effectively to the right groups.
- Enable root cause analysis and effective trending of support request data.
- Enable automatic assignment of priorities.
- Enhance the search capabilities of the knowledge base.
- Use consistent categorization across knowledge base, incident and problem management systems.
- Ensure that naming is consistent with configuration database scheme.

Common Problems With Classification Schemes

Common problems with non-maintained category trees include:
- **Duplicate descriptions:** Category names may be different but describe the same thing, as in "printing" and "printers." This creates confusion in both categorizing the support request as it is recorded and in reporting.
- **Unused/overused categories:** Categories that are not being

---

[6] Jennifer Streitwieser, "Designing Categories for Business Benefit" (Available on the HDI web site, www.thinkhdi.com/publications/whitePapers/)

used are prime candidates for deletion or revision. They are just taking up space and making it difficult to find the useful types. Similarly, low-level categories (at the symptom level) that are being used too much indicate the possibility that more categories are needed to segment the data more instructively. The "other" bucket is a commonly over-used category. This, by the way, is not a bad category except if it is unmanaged. You can never anticipate all the support requests that will arise in technical support, and "other" is a needed element. However, the support center should be monitoring the use of that category on a regular, probably weekly, basis to ensure that types are properly identified.

- **Unintuitive structure:** It is unclear to support analysts how to categorize problems. This can be due to type names that are not descriptive or tree structures that have become jumbled over time. It may be that technical terms are used rather than terms that might be used by an end-user. End-user terms are more relevant in this instance.

- **Inconsistent types and levels:** This structure is characterized by lower levels (e.g.: symptom level) of different branches of the category tree having dissimilar elements, or different descriptions of the same symptom. Additionally, some branches of the category tree may have two levels, while others have three. Inconsistency creates confusion.

- **Too many:** Especially in higher levels, too many categories are confusing to the analyst.

Classification Levels

In most support centers, three levels of classification are used to describe the support requests received. Three category levels generally provide enough information about the support request but do not burden the support analyst with too much classification activity. One of the problems with classification schemes identified above was inconsistent levels of classification. Think hard before creating any categories that deviate from the standard three levels. As noted, the inconsistency is jarring to analysts and creates anomalies in reporting and other actions predicated on the classification.

Your service management system may default to names for the classification levels. For example, the system might use category, sub-category and action, or category, type and item (CTI). In this discussion, we will refer to the classification levels as problem type, category and symptom.

The problem type describes the broad areas for which you provide service. In a technical support environment, these areas usually are platforms, applications and systems such as hardware, software, network, etc. The category describes the specific item within the broad problem type. Together, the problem type and category answer the

In most support centers, three levels of classification are used to describe the support requests received.

question, "To what configuration item does this support request pertain?"

The symptom describes what exactly was wrong with the specific item, such as password reset, reporting issue or a malfunction. This could also include how-to questions, which are not really a symptom but are a reason for the support request. The symptom answers the question, "What was wrong with this item?"

The symptom descriptions can be similar across many problem type/category combinations because they describe the action taken on the specific item. In ITIL terms, symptoms can describe both failures in the infrastructure and support requests, such as delivery requests or how-to's. For example, a list of all symptoms might include these items:

- Malfunction
- Replaced
- Password reset

- How-to
- Documentation request
- Move/add/change

Obviously, "password reset" will not apply to most hardware problems but will apply to some applications. It is for this reason that a matrix approach to assigning symptom is best, as in the following example:

How to Create Categories

1. Make a list of problem types and categories. Remember, problem and categories are descriptions of what configuration item is having the problem or is in question. Keep in mind these important issues:

   - How you want reports to look and how you would like them to be sorted and structured.
   - How escalation rules will apply. You may need to structure these categories according to the escalation groups available to you. For example, there may be an application analyst who deals only with proprietary software. How will you classify support requests so you can automatically assign problems to this person?

Problem/ categories	Hardware/ printer	Hardware/ laptop	Software/ OS	Software/ accounting
Symptoms				
Malfunction	✓	✓		
Replaced	✓	✓		
Password reset			✓	✓
How-to			✓	✓
Move/add/change	✓	✓	✓	✓

   - Do we need more than two levels of categories to describe the configuration item? If yes, then expand to three levels, understanding that this will place a burden on the support analysts who record the support requests.

2. Assemble the problem and categories into a hierarchy that

represents the top two levels of a category tree. You can create a simple spreadsheet that shows the one-to-many relationship between the first and second levels of the tree.

3. Make a list of the symptoms that describe the nature of the support request. Start by thinking of these symptoms independently of the configuration items they might link to. Consider the level of granularity needed for symptoms. For example, is the symptom "reset" sufficient to describe what was wrong, or do you need both "password reset" and "hardware reset" to describe the difference between password requests and modem requests? Making one list of symptoms ensures that you have consistent descriptions across all problem/categories types.

4. Complete the matrix that coordinates problem/categories with symptoms, as in the previous example. You can add to the spreadsheet you created.

5. Enter the matrix into the service management system.

Considerations

Do not try to anticipate every detail as you start. It is better to start simply and add complexity later. Creating a process for making changes to the category trees will ensure that future changes will be rational ones.

Where will you put an "other" category – only in the symptom level, or in the problem/categories level?

Do you find that you need other levels of categories, either in the description of the item in question or in the symptom of the support request? It is OK to combine two levels into one level. For example, you may find that you want to group your symptoms into two main groups of "service requests" and "failures" to comply with ITIL language. In this case, you would list the proper heading first, followed by the actual action taken, like this:

- Service request, how-to
- Service request, documentation request
- Service request, password reset

- Service request, move/add/change
- Failure, break-fix
- Failure, bug
- Failure, replace

You may wish to use the escalation matrix on page 87, which is included in the accompanying resource CD (to purchase, see information at the end of this book), to help you map the escalation groups to the categories that you set up. Think of all of the groups to which support requests are escalated and enter them in this matrix. Then work backward to create the proper categorization. You must have an escalation path for each combination of categories.

Using a Card Sort Exercise

Once you get all your values identified, you want to make sure that your category tree is organized in an intuitive manner. This will help to ensure that the analysts properly code each incoming support request. A good way to do that, and to involve your analysts in this effort, is to do a "card sort" exercise. Using index cards, write each value from your category schema on a card. With the value, note to which category level it belongs. For example, you would create one card for hardware, which is a problem category, and would note on the card "problem type" or "level 1." You might even color-code the cards by category level to provide visual prompts for sorting and ensuring accuracy. Next, let analysts take their deck of cards to a large table and sort them in ways that make sense to them. The analysts should create a tree structure that represents the way they would like to see the categories in the service management system. The coordinator of this exercise records each person's preferences and creates a tree structure that conforms to the rules of the majority. One way to record the results of this exercise is to photograph each card sort.

A good way to involve your analysts in this effort is to do a "card sort" exercise.

Support Center Escalation Paths by Symptom

Customer/policy support requests	Second-level	Third-level
Angry customer	Email: Phone: Pager/Cell:	Email: Phone: Pager/Cell:
New employee issues	Email: Phone: Pager/Cell:	Email: Phone: Pager/Cell:
Terminated employee procedure	Email: Phone: Pager/Cell:	Email: Phone: Pager/Cell:
Policy issues	Email: Phone: Pager/Cell:	Email: Phone: Pager/Cell:
Hardware/LAN	**Second-level**	**Third-level**
User cannot connect	Email: Phone: Pager/Cell:	Email: Phone: Pager/Cell:
New account setup	Email: Phone: Pager/Cell:	Email: Phone: Pager/Cell:
Password re-set	Email: Phone: Pager/Cell:	Email: Phone: Pager/Cell:
New printer configuration	Email: Phone: Pager/Cell:	Email: Phone: Pager/Cell:
Hardware/desktops	**Second-level**	**Third-level**
Image problems	Email: Phone: Pager/Cell:	Email: Phone: Pager/Cell:
Image changes	Email: Phone: Pager/Cell:	Email: Phone: Pager/Cell:
New machine name	Email: Phone: Pager/Cell:	Email: Phone: Pager/Cell:
Delete machine name	Email: Phone: Pager/Cell:	Email: Phone: Pager/Cell:
Laptop problems	Email: Phone: Pager/Cell:	Email: Phone: Pager/Cell:
Etc.		

After completing the card sort to ensure the intuitive nature of the categories, it is time to finish the spreadsheet of problem types, categories and symptoms and to input it into the service management system.

Best Practices – Support Request Handling Processes

1. The support center logs all support requests in the service management system. Some mechanism is set up in the service management system to expedite the documentation of short calls.
2. Notifications are created to ensure the timely handling of all support requests.
3. Categories within the service management system are regularly reviewed for relevance and efficiency and are updated regularly.
4. Document your support request handling methods using both flowcharts and formal documentation

Chapter Six: Knowledge Management

PUNDITS TELL US that we live in the post-industrial information economy. The majority of the business world now runs on information instead of on natural resources such as steel and rubber. However, information itself is not that useful to us. Anyone who has used Google knows that most of what is presented after a search is irrelevant and useless to the seeker. It is information that is packaged into usable, applicable and relevant knowledge that is most valuable to the seeker and especially to the support center. Knowledge management is the process that helps us create and maintain relevant knowledge.

The Knowledge Management Process

As technology specialists, we all have a tendency to believe that our job security depends on the amount of knowledge we know, retain and hoard (or keep to ourselves). After all, isn't the know-it-all employee indispensable to a company? Unfortunately, this is no longer true. Layoffs, downsizing and outsourcing prove that no one is indispensable, regardless of the amount of knowledge a person retains. Perhaps because of layoffs, downsizing and outsourcing, the tendency to hoard knowledge persists. It is up to the support manager to create a culture of knowledge-sharing by rewarding behaviors that teach others and deepen their expertise. Especially when a support center implements customer self-service, it is imperative that the analysts learn to document and share knowledge.

The support center that does not embrace a structured knowledge management process is going to be an expensive one. Knowledge-sharing saves money – and **Knowledge-sharing saves money.** what support center is not under intense pressure to do that? Knowledge management ensures that each analyst has access to the latest wisdom of the group regarding problem-solving and can actually reduce the time to proficiency, or the time a new hire must spend in formal training. It can also boost first contact resolution rates, which reduce costs and increase customer satisfaction. Lastly, knowledge that is shared with the customers via a web-based knowledge base can save money by off-loading human-mediated support requests to self-service. A customer knowledge base can save customers' time and can extend the support center's virtual hours to 24/7 without having to pay analysts to work those hours.

An approach to knowledge management that is gaining approval in the support community is Knowledge-Centered Support (KCS). This approach, created by a consortium of large technology companies that sought a standard knowledge process, enables problem-solving and knowledge-sharing. The Consortium for Service Innovation's web site is www.serviceinnovation.org, where you can find resources such as white papers to help you understand more about Knowledge-Centered Support. The basic concepts of KCS are:

- Knowledge should be captured in the workflow, not at some future time.
- All knowledge solutions should be structured consistently.
- Knowledge should be immediately shared with all support center analysts, even if it is unedited or incomplete. Others in the support center can contribute to the solution's completion.
- Once you view a solution, you must use it, fix it or flag it for someone else to fix. If you do not find a solution, you add it.
- The quality of the knowledge base is everyone's responsibility.
- Knowledge solutions are shared with the customers based on re-use within the support center.
- Analysts are judged on the quality of their contributions.[7]

The knowledge management process must begin with the structure of a knowledge solution. In the best support centers, all knowledge solutions conform to a standard structure, such as:

- Problem description
- Environment (the software and hardware products in which the problem occurs)
- Cause
- Resolution (steps taken to resolve the problem)
- History/audit trail (author, date, revision dates, revision authors)

These sections are typically a sub-set of the entire support request record in a service management system. Environment needs to be included because a problem may occur in several products. In some simple knowledge bases, the analyst may have to add cause and resolution as headers within a description text field.

The process for creating and reviewing knowledge is important in the support center. It is outside of the scope of this book to teach KCS concepts, but the process advocated here is based on

---

[7] *Consortium for Service Innovation, "Knowledge Management Foundations: KCS Principles Workshop," 2004, 2005*

Knowledge-Centered Support concepts.

In order to implement a knowledge process effectively, the role of knowledge manager must be assigned to a senior member of the support center. This person is responsible for coaching analysts in effective solution creation, analyzing solutions shared in the support center to identify the solutions to publish to the customer's knowledge base, and reviewing the knowledge base for archival material.

The process starts with the analyst who recognizes a new problem or realizes that no solution exists for this problem. As the analyst solves and documents the problem, she is doing so with a

The process starts with the analyst. mind to sharing the documentation as a solution. Once the interaction is over, she publishes the solution to the knowledge base and the solution is immediately available to her colleagues. As other analysts come across the same problem, they may add information to the problem. For example, an analyst discovers another product that the problem is affecting and he adds that product to the environment list. Other analysts may also correct the information in the solution with new findings about the problem.

On a regular basis, the knowledge manager reviews solutions created by each analyst. Although this is done on a random basis, the knowledge manager must ensure that a minimum number of solutions are reviewed for each analyst monthly. After reviewing the solution and completing an evaluation form, the knowledge manager coaches the analyst to improve the clarity of his writing, the format, and the content of the solution.

The form used to evaluate a solution and coach the analyst might look like the one on the right.

Note that the form includes 12 criteria of an acceptable solution. The goal for the group may be set to greater than 90 percent, which Jane did not achieve in her first solution review but met or

Solution /Quality Evaluation Form

Analyst:	Jane									
Solution number:	12345	12349	13425							
Review date:	2/1/2007	2/15/2007	2/22/2007							
Coach:	Renee	Renee	Greg							
Criteria:										
1. Duplicate	1									
2. Too little content										
3. Compound			1							
4. Not to Standard										
5. Incorrect fix										
6. Environment mixed with problem description										
7. Custom/ installation specific	1									
8. Solution attributes incorrect										
9. Link does not work										
10. Audience inappropriate										
11. Followed structure										
12. Title describes solution										
Total incorrects:	2	0	1	0	0	0	0	0	0	
Score:	83%	100%	92%	100%	100%	100%	100%	100%	100%	

exceeded in subsequent reviews. This suggests that Renee, the coach, discussed the shortcomings of the first solution with Jane, and now Jane is equipped to create quality solutions.

The knowledge manager is in charge of publishing new solutions

Analyst re-use indicates the usefulness of the solution's content.

to the customer knowledge base. This is done based on which solutions are accessed most frequently by the support analysts. Analyst re-use indicates the usefulness of the solution's content.

The knowledge manager periodically reviews the knowledge base for solutions that are redundant, out of date or have no re-use records and archives those solutions.

Some ways to encourage knowledge-sharing through this process are to every month publish the names of the authors of the most frequently accessed knowledge solutions. The analyst monthly report displays the quantity of new solutions created for each analyst, plus the knowledge base quality score and re-use rates. This encourages participation in the process. Some support centers create periodic competitions for usage of the knowledge base. For example, they award a prize for the person who wins the most frequently accessed solution for the month.

A knowledge management process applicable to smaller support centers looks like this:

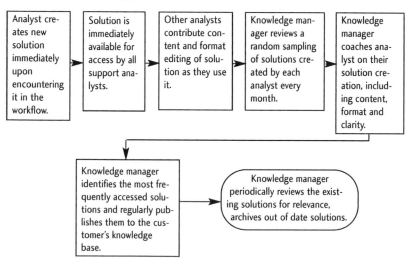

Knowledge Management Process

In order to expedite handling customer support requests on shrink-wrapped software products such as Microsoft Office and Adobe, some support centers purchase knowledge packs from a third-party vendor. These packages of pre-written knowledge are immediately available for use in your knowledge base or by using the vendor's knowledge base. This is a way to reduce the costs by offering self-service capabilities on commercially available software.

Best Practices – Knowledge Management

1 Knowledge is most useful when it is first discovered; therefore, knowledge management processes must ensure that support analysts have access to knowledge immediately.
2. Knowledge is by nature messy and evolves over time.
3. Collaboration in the support center ensures better knowledge.
4. Each analyst is responsible for the quality of the knowledge base.
5. Analysts can be coached to improve their solution creation quality.

## CHAPTER SEVEN

Support Tools

EVERY SUPPORT CENTER needs tools that enable efficient service delivery. In this chapter, we will explore the tools that the smaller support center needs and discuss the features of each. Fortunately, the support center industry has matured to the point that many tools are available at reasonable prices. All support centers now have access to the basic tools.

Because vendors and their products change so quickly, please refer to KR Consulting's web site at www.krconsulting.com for an up-to-date list of products for the smaller support center.

Service Management System

This tool was formerly referred to as a call tracking system, but the functionality of the products in this category has increased to include many other aspects of service delivery, such as configuration management, change or asset management, and workflow engines. "Service management system" is now a more descriptive title. Other names commonly used for this tool are case resolution system, incident/problem management system, ticket management system, etc.

Every support center needs a service management system to record the support requests received, to provide a history of service **Every support center needs a service management system.** provided by customer and to document the work being performed in the center. Without a service management system, the support center cannot be effective, so this tool must be the first purchase that a new center makes. A smaller support center can function without an ACD phone system and many of the other tools listed in this chapter, but not without a service management system.

Benefits of a service management system include:

- Recording the number and nature of support requests received.
- Tracking and reporting on support requests, such as number of requests received by category, by priority, by analyst, by day, etc.
- Automating workflow and business rules, such as notifications.
- Providing metrics with which to manage the support center.
- Providing a history of customers' contacts with the support center.

Service management systems can be integrated with several other tools, such as the phone system, the knowledge base system, a service monitoring system or a network monitoring system. Integration of any type used to be financially out of reach for smaller support centers, but the advent of newer technologies such as VoIP and the increasing functionality found in products marketed to the SMB (small and mid-sized business) market make it possible for more support centers to enjoy the benefits of more-integrated support tools.

Basic requirements of a service management system include:

- Ability to record support requests, including the following data:
  o Customer demographics and profile of equipment and products owned.
  o Product and environment of the support request.
  o Categorization of the support request.
  o Problem description/resolution steps field.
- Time tracking to calculate work time.
- Notification and escalation features.
  o Flexible email notifications triggered by events.
  o SLA guideline notification (e.g.: a ticket is about to breach a response-time commitment, and a notification is sent to the analyst and the senior analyst).
- Status codes for different phases in the life cycle of the support request.
- Knowledge base features.
  o Ability to link support request to kb solutions.
  o Ability to designate internal (private) solutions versus external (public) solutions.
  o Complete audit trail of who has modified the solution.
  o Strong search capability.
  o Ability to structure all solutions consistently.
- For external support centers.
  o Ability to access both sales and support databases.
  o Ability to convert sales records to customer records and retain the sales history.
  o Ability to convert sales records to customer records and retain the sales history.
  o Defect tracking and enhancement request tracking (could be

in the same database but with flags that differentiate records).
- For internal support centers.
    o Ability to convert incidents to problem management entries.
    o Interface with configuration management/asset management system.

The Build Versus Buy Decision

Should the support center build a service management system that is customized to its needs, or should it purchase a commercially available one? In today's market, there is little benefit in making a build decision for a service management system. There are so many flexible yet inexpensive tools on the market that no support center should be using its precious internal resources to program a service management system from scratch or to cobble a system together using shareware components. Given the cost of employees' time, it is far cheaper in the end to purchase a commercially available system that another company updates and supports than to write and maintain your own. Start with a tool that fits your budget, configure it to the extent it allows and modify your processes to what it can do, if you must.

There is little benefit in making a build decision for a service management system.

I have seen many support centers that use service management systems programmed in-house and maintained by one technical person. Invariably, management worries that the proverbial bus will hit the lone programmer, leaving the support center with no one to maintain its system. Also in these companies, it is often difficult to get changes made to internally developed systems because it diverts a programmer's focus from product development efforts. When everything is considered regarding building the system in-house, the cost in terms of employees' time is greater than purchasing a commercially available tool.

Please see KR Consulting's web site for a list of service management systems for the smaller support center.

ACD

An automatic call distribution (ACD) telephone system allows the caller to be directed to the next available analyst or to the analyst who has been available the longest. In traditional telephone systems, the ACD was an add-on function to the company's PBX (public branch exchange) system (the telephone system that allows a company to have one main phone number with many extensions). An ACD today can be an add-on to the PBX, or it can be its own unit that accepts calls directly.

In addition to enabling flexible call routing options, an important reason to consider an ACD for the smaller support center is to track metrics on telephone activity. With an ACD, the support manager is able to measure the following:

- Number of calls that arrive every 30 minutes (referred to as the call arrival pattern).
- Average length of time it takes an analyst to answer the phone (this is expressed either as average speed of answer or service level).
- Abandon rate (the percentage of calls in which the customer hangs up before speaking to an analyst).
- Length of time that the analyst spends on the phone and in after-call work time/wrap-up time (average handle time).
- Number of calls taken by an analyst.

Many times, smaller support centers are not aware that their company's PBX has basic ACD capabilities.

Many times, smaller support centers are not aware that their company's PBX has basic ACD capabilities inherent in it. Some centers are able to implement ACD functions with a small investment of funds to "turn on" the ACD. Beware that some of these simple ACDs have constraints that impede their use, such as not providing access to the metrics except through a printout or not being able to export the data from the "black box" of the ACD. Even in those cases, however, it may be useful to turn on the ACD features just to enable a more equitable distribution of calls to the analysts in the support center.

The advent of Voice over Internet Protocol (VoIP) telephony has broken down the wall between data systems and traditional telephone systems – the telephone system is now a data system. These systems can be called server-based telephony because they now run on a computer server and use the data network to convey telephone conversations, via data packets, to the analyst's phone. Some vendors that cater to the SMB market are now offering service management systems that integrate to VoIP phone systems and are priced attractively for the smaller organization.

Many smaller support centers get along without an ACD. These centers typically use the dispatch method of handling support requests (see discussion in Chapter Four: Support Request Handling Methods) and use only the functions of the company's PBX phone system. Other support centers use the PBX hunt group feature, which searches for an analyst in the support center in a predefined order, or they might program the phone system to ring all the analysts' telephones at once until an analyst answers or the caller is directed to voicemail. These systems are adequate for some small centers, and if the financial resources are just not available for anything more advanced, the support center gets along with what is available. These support centers lack the metrics and the equitable distribution of calls that an ACD offers.

When I managed a support center of about 25 analysts, I was able to justify the purchase of an ACD, which in those days represented a rather large investment. Before the implementation of the ACD, the company's receptionist would take messages from customers for callbacks from an analyst. This method became inefficient as the support center grew; customers started complaining that they did not receive callbacks in a timely manner or at all. After reviewing the cost justification study that I created that quantified savings in terms of higher productivity of the support center, the final word from the CEO was, "If it makes the customers stop complaining about not getting a call back, let's do it!"

Knowledge Base

A knowledge base is a necessity for today's support center, no matter the size. The good news is that most commercially available service management systems today have some level of knowledge base built into the product. This is music to the ears of the smaller support center manager, who definitely cannot afford the price tag of the major knowledge base products. What is sometimes lacking in the knowledge bases that are integrated into the service management system are advanced search capabilities and features such as linking a knowledge solution to a support request record, or recording a complete history of who has edited the solution.

Good news! Most commercially available service management systems have built-in knowledge bases.

As an accompaniment to the knowledge base, some internal support centers purchase pre-packaged knowledge on shrink-wrapped software titles such as Microsoft Office applications. This practice jump-starts the knowledge base and can serve as a handy reference for support analysts, too.

Instant Messaging and Web Chat

Instant messaging (IM) among support analysts is a boon to collaboration and can increase first contact resolutions and decrease resolution times in the center. Several warnings about this communication are in order: If the analysts use an outside IM service such as Yahoo or AOL, there is no security of the information being shared because the message passes outside of the company's firewall. Another warning is that unless you are using an advanced tool, there is no record of the interactions on instant messaging. This can be of little to no concern if everyone understands that it is a fleeting form of communication.

Web chat is another matter. Web chat is typically offered to customers by large organizations. On their web sites, they offer customers the opportunity to click a button and start a chat session with a support analyst. This technology can **Web chat is a synchronous form of communication.** be alluring, but the wise support manager will look carefully before leaping. Keep in mind that web chat is a synchronous form of communication, which means that an analyst must be available to chat with the customer whenever the customer wishes. Offering chat as a communication medium must be managed exactly like telephone calls, which means that the support center must, in a sense, over-staff in order to have enough people available to answer the chat requests in a timely fashion. If a support center is having trouble responding quickly to telephone calls, it has no business offering web chat. Web chat is best deployed in organizations that purchase a universal queuing ACD system that distributes all communication media to the analysts. These systems will deliver a telephone call, an electronic support request, a fax or a chat session to the next available analyst. For now, these advanced systems carry a price tag that is out of the reach of smaller support centers. Web chat is generally not a good idea for small support centers.

Remote Control

It is costly for a support center to lack a remote control capability. Remote control allows analysts to connect to the customer's computer and see what the customer is seeing. Resolutions in the support center increase while costs decrease. For internal support centers, remote control enables them to resolve more support requests without a costly desk-side visit. For external support centers, it enables first-level analysts to resolve more support requests on the first contact. Remote control can also provide an opportunity to educate the customer and make that customer more independent of the support center in the future. Although the lack of a remote control tool is not a showstopper, all support centers can benefit from its availability

Remote control allows analysts to connect to the customer's computer.

Survey Tools

Many service management systems today have a built-in customer survey function that integrates the support request data with survey data. Usually, the survey instrument is a web-form and the service management system automatically sends email invitations to the survey with a link to the survey web site. Data is gathered into the service management system's database, and managers can run reports from there.

If an independent web survey tool is needed, there are many inexpensive web-based survey tools available. Please refer to www.krconsulting.com for an updated list of possible vendors. As with the service management systems' survey tool, these web-based tools send an email invitation to the customer with a link to a web-based survey form. Data and reporting are

There are many inexpensive web-based survey tools available.

done on the tool's database, making this a second choice due to the lack of integration between survey tool and service management system. Because these systems are so economical to use, many smaller support centers use them for employee satisfaction surveys in addition to customer surveys.

Lastly, a growing number of mid-sized support centers are using telephone-based IVR (interactive voice response) survey tools. At the end of the support call, the analyst asks the customer if she would like to be transferred to the phone survey. The IVR offers the customer a survey, and voice and touch-tone responses are recorded. It can be more difficult to review all the recorded comments delivered through the telephone survey system, but most support centers find that the response rate is greater than the email-based web surveys.

Call Recording

Traditionally, call recording systems were too expensive and considered frivolous investments for smaller support centers. As discussed in Chapter Ten: Quality Assurance, all support centers should do some sort of service monitoring, even if it is only a ticket review. Call recording systems for large support centers typically are integrated with the telephone system, capture and record all calls, or allow the manager to program a time block in which to record calls. When I managed a large call center for a financial services firm, all calls were recorded and the recordings were kept for years because of compliance requirements.

Today, expensive call recording systems offer much more than just call recording. These systems are now digital and can record both the audio and the computer key-entry portion of a service interaction, then play both back for a manager. Today's systems can offer a customizable service monitoring evaluation form and storage database with full reporting capabilities. Some systems even integrate with training applets that can be pushed to the analyst's computer when they are not taking calls. These advanced features are not even within the realm of imagination for smaller support centers, but features are continually being pushed down-market, and the new VoIP telephone systems enable integration of call recording with the ACD.

For the small support center without a VoIP solution, there are analogue and digital options for recording calls. Both ways assume that the manager has the ability to monitor analysts' calls through their extension. Most ACDs offer this capability, but regular PBX phone systems may not. The analogue option is a low-tech, inexpensive system of recording calls. For less than US$100, the support center can purchase a small tape recorder or digital recorder from a local electronics store and connect it to the manager's phone. The manager loads a tape into the recorder (if it is not digital), logs into the supervisor capability on the phone, starts listening to an analyst and then walks away from the phone to let it record a morning's worth of phone calls of that particular analyst. The digital option uses a software program that connects to a regular telephone via an adaptor and records the telephone conversation on the computer. The digital systems have advanced features such as voice detection that turns on the system

For the small support center, there are analog and digital options.

when sound is heard and turns off when there is silence on the extension. Whatever system you use to record calls, the manager later listens to the calls and continues through the service monitoring process.

Other Tools

Network and other systems monitoring tools alert the support center to problems with the system before the customer calls. Some support centers integrate the monitoring system with the service management system, which enables the automatic generation of support request tickets when something on the network malfunctions. Because the health of a network is so vital to even a smaller organization, access to this technology is more common than not in smaller internal support centers.

Password reset technology is an important tool for the internal IT department and can dramatically reduce the number of support requests the support center receives. Technically, password reset is a tool for avoiding calls, not a tool for delivering support per se, and is therefore out of the scope of this book. Password reset technology, once implemented, is a boon to the support center.

Process for Purchasing New Technology Tools

Any organization should follow a disciplined process to identify and purchase new tools. Although smaller support centers rarely create in-depth requests for proposals (RFPs), conduct bidders' conferences or pore over numerous, lengthy vendor proposals, a streamlined process ensures that the support center gets what it needs from a new purchase.

The process looks like the example on the next page.

Research the Market

The support manager or his designate starts by researching the

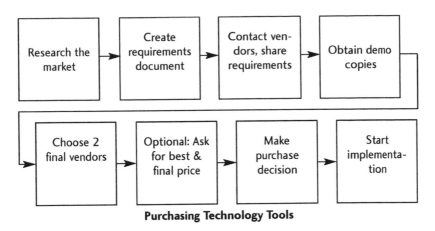

Purchasing Technology Tools

market. Web sites that offer lists of vendors, such as www.krconsulting.com, www.thinkhdi.com, www.callcentermagazine.com and www.theresourcecenter.com, should be the first stop on this journey. Contacting colleagues in the support industry to ask them what they use or recommend is also a good step to take. Once you have a list of possible vendors, visit each vendor's web site to gather more information. Often you can download entire brochures, product specifications and even demonstration copies of the software from the web site. The purpose of this step is to become educated about the features available on the market and likely vendors. If you contact a salesperson at this step, you can expect him to try to influence the next several steps. It may be better to wait to make contact with salespeople until after you have written requirements.

Create a Requirements Document

The next step, the most important one, is to create a business requirements document for the new tool. The support manager may wish to gather a team of analysts to help brainstorm requirements, or at least have some analysts review the requirements once they are written. In business terms,

Create a business requirements document for the new tool.

not technical language, the requirements document describes what the new tool needs to accomplish for the support center. It should include:

- Hardware requirements
- OS platform
- Database requirements
- Cost range
- System performance
- Features
- Usability requirements
- Reporting
- Internal security

The requirements document details what is important for the support center and will guide the subsequent steps of this process. Without it, a support center can be mesmerized by vendors' latest bells and whistles that may not be that important to your operations.

An optional activity is to prioritize the requirements list into "must haves" and "nice to haves" and/or assign weights to each category or feature. This step usually validates what the manager knows intuitively. Prioritizing requirements makes the support center define what is most important to the operation.

Caveat: Do not let vendor salespeople get involved in this step, as they will shape the requirements to what they offer. You did market research to determine what features are generally available and to obviate the need for a salesperson until the next step.

Contact Vendors and Share Requirements With Them/ Obtain Demo Copies

After requirements are written, it is now time to share the requirements with salespeople from the vendors you identified in the market research step. Ask them to read your requirements and make comments, either in a conversation in which you take notes or via a written response. You are interviewing the company at this point, so be sure to inquire about its support center and support services. Obtain demo copies of the product, if possible, and let your support analysts test it in-house. Gather their feedback.

At this point, you may wish to prepare a spreadsheet to compare the products. This spreadsheet helps you select the vendor that best meets your needs. List the major requirements as rows and the competing vendors as columns. Score each vendor using a numeric scale (1 to 3 or 1 to 5) according to how well the solution meets your needs. By completing this matrix, the top two vendors will have the highest score at the bottom.

Choose Two Finalist Vendors/Ask for Best and Final Price

The reasons for choosing two final vendors are to have a fallback position if something happens in the last moments of negotiations and to try to get a better price by playing each vendor off the other. You can tell the vendors that you have narrowed it down to two finalists and then ask if they would like to make a best and final offer. Some vendors in this space do not have a lot of room to discount prices, but it is always prudent to ask. The winner is the one with the best price and best features for your needs.

Best Practices — Support Tools

1. Each support center should have a service management system in which to record support requests. There are many affordable systems on the market today.

2. An ACD is a luxury for some small support centers, but it enables the tracking of metrics that are otherwise not available and creates a more equitable distribution of calls as compared to a hunt group or round-robin system.

3. Every support center should have some form of a web-based knowledge management tool. The good news is that most service management systems incorporate a knowledge management tool of some sort.

4. Instant messaging is important for communications within the support center. Web chat with customers, however, can be problematic for support centers that cannot afford universal queuing technology that distributes chat sessions along with telephone calls and electronic requests.

5. Remote control tools are important for any size support center because they allow analysts to solve more support requests.

6. In purchasing any new support tool, the most important step is to identify the business requirements independently of a vendor.

## CHAPTER EIGHT

Support Web Site

DOING MORE WITH LESS. Call avoidance. Self-service. Reducing costs of support. You have heard all these executive mandates before – no support manager is immune from feeling the pressure to minimize expenses. This is where a robust support web site comes to the rescue. The support web site can offer services that need no human intervention, can virtually extend the support center's hours of operation and can provide an access method that is preferred by a segment of the customer base.

Both internal and external support centers can find helpful information on creating effective support web sites in the Association of Support Professionals' annual "The Ten Best Web Support Sites"[8] report. This report offers a wealth of cutting-edge information on what the best support centers are doing to create effective self-service web sites. Each winner of the competition presents a narrative of the biggest challenges faced in creating the web site, a description of the main features and the lessons learned.

Effective support web sites have common features, such as:

---

[8] Association of Support Professionals, "The Ten Best Web Support Sites," www.asponline.com/awards.html

- Home page for either the IT department or the support center that lists information such as the support center's phone number and operating hours, and current performance statistics such as response time, mean time to resolve, customer satisfaction measures, etc.
- A web version of the support guide or overview of the service level agreement. This helps to set customer expectations and gives both analysts and customers easy access to the information.
- Access to frequently asked questions or hot topics.
- Access to a knowledge base with search capabilities.
- Ability to enter support requests through a web-form.
- Ability to download product updates and documentation.

For internal support centers, the following items could be considered for the support web site.

- List of all support center employees with their pictures and biographical sketches. External support centers may not wish to publish this information to people outside the company.
- Ability to enter move/add/change requests, new hires and loaner requests through online forms with business rules for routing approval requests.

The main features will be explored in the following sections. At the end of this chapter, we will discuss ways to encourage customers to use these features.

Knowledge Base and FAQs

As mentioned in Chapter Seven: Support Tools, a knowledge base feature is usually included in service management systems for the small to medium-sized support center. Once the support center has a collection of solutions that have been used at least three times by support analysts, you can offer access to the public portion of the knowledge base to customers. A spectacular support center will not post a knowledge base to customers until internal knowledge processes are running well and a critical mass of solutions has been created and re-used multiple times. Remember that requirements for a knowledge base include the ability to count the re-uses of a solution and to identify the audience (i.e.: only the support center or the support center and the customer) that is allowed to see a solution.

Once the quality and breadth of the knowledge is confirmed and the customer interface on the web is enabled, some support centers have successfully launched their knowledge base in stealth mode, meaning they do not publicize the knowledge base but wait for customers to find it. This works especially well for internal support centers whose customers may not be as technically savvy and self-service hungry as external support centers' customers might be. These support centers gather feedback on the use of the knowledge base from the accidental users by sending surveys to the users and even interviewing them in person. After revising the knowledge base, the support center makes an official announcement of the service and launches its web site marketing campaign.

Some support centers have successfully launched their knowledge base in stealth mode.

Some support web sites offer two ways to get to knowledge solutions: through a search engine that prompts the user to enter a word or phrase, or through a menu that allows the customer to drill down to the knowledge solution. This dual access approach acknowledges that customers have different ways of categorizing or expressing what knowledge they are seeking and provides contrasting ways to find information.

Web-Based Support Request Entry

Most service management systems also provide a mechanism through which customers can enter support requests into a web-form. The support request is immediately populated into the service management system, where it can be dispatched to an analyst for processing. As mentioned previously, offering a web-form is much more effective than accepting free-form email support requests because the support center can require the customer to enter data that allows the support analyst to begin troubleshooting immediately. The web-form might prompt the customer for details including:

- Customer's name and location (if the web site does not require login and password for access).
- Product name, module and version number.
- Operating system or platform.
- Priority of the support request (support centers that also provide phone support should educate customers to use the telephone if the support request is critical or urgent).
- Full description of the problem or request.

The user interface for the web-form should also allow customers to search their existing support requests and add new information if applicable.

Some support centers respond to electronic support requests via the support web site, with an email notification to the customer when a new entry is available. Other support centers initiate a telephone conversation with the customer once the customer has submitted a support request electronically. Others communicate via email exclusively. The demands and situations of your customers and the environment within the support center will dictate which response method you use.

Electronic submission is not a self-service option. One thing to remember is that electronic submission is not a self-service option. An analyst must respond to the support request and work it just like a telephone call. However, this method is more efficient than telephone or chat support in terms of headcount because it is a delayed (asynchronous) form of communication. It is also more efficient than free-form email support because it requires the customer to enter enough information so that the analyst can start the troubleshooting process upon receipt of the support request.

Product and Documentation Downloads

For both internal and external support centers, giving customers the ability to independently access and download product updates and documentation means that the support center does not have to handle these issues. External support centers work with their developers and technical writers to offer these downloads to customers. Some companies find that some software downloads are too big to send electronically, and these companies may still have to mail physical media to their customers. All documentation should be downloadable. Internal support centers work with their development partners to provide product updates either through the support web site or through automatic pushes of updates directly to the desktop. If the IT organization mandates a standard image for all the desktops, then software update pushes are considered mandatory in today's market.

Forums and Other Self-Help

Many support web sites offer customers the opportunity to collaborate with other customers through a forum or threaded discussion group. The customers post questions and other customers provide answers. In its purest form, the support forum is strictly customer-to-customer support. However, some support centers monitor support forums by assigning one support analyst the responsibility of reviewing all posted answers for accuracy. In some forums, you see entries from a support analyst that correct a previous answer. The support centers that monitor the forums want to ensure that accurate answers are provided.

Some companies identify the most frequent contributors to the forum.

In any case, this is a cost-effective service-delivery method for the support center. In addition, many customers enjoy giving advice to others and receive intrinsic rewards from doing so. In order to encourage the use of forums, some companies identify the most frequent contributors to the forum and make them feel special by posting their pictures, qualifications and number of support answers on the web site.

Automated Request Entry for Internal Support Centers

Moves/adds/changes (MACs) are common support requests in an internal IT environment. In the past these requests were all handled manually using paper forms. However, most service management systems today enable the support center to automate much of the process. Automating this process provides an opportunity to save time and effort.

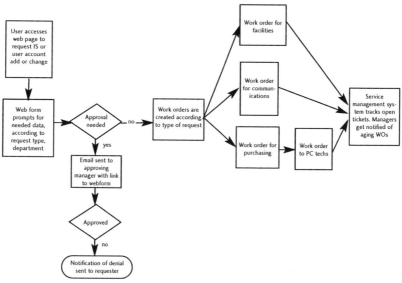

This process is usually implemented with a combination of the service management system's innate capabilities and custom web programming.

The user accesses a web-form on the company Intranet and requests the new equipment or new hire by completing the form. If approval is needed, an email notification is sent to the approving manager, with a link to the web-form. When approval is granted, the system creates work orders in the service management system, which are sent to the appropriate group's queue with a deadline for completion. Most service management systems allow managers to monitor open work orders.

Marketing the Support Web Site

Now that you have built the support web site, will customers come? Usually no, unless you mount a marketing campaign that repeatedly emphasizes the benefits of its use. Here are some ways that support centers market their web site:

- Communicate on an ongoing basis to customers about the existence and benefits of the support web site. This can be done through newsletters, posters, tri-fold brochures, business cards printed just for the web site, email signatures, gifts such as a mouse pad printed with the URL of the web site on it, etc.. Some internal support centers set up a table in the company cafeteria and pass out brochures and gifts to publicize the web site.

- When the knowledge base is mature and you have confidence that most support requests are documented there, have analysts walk each caller through the knowledge base to find the answer to the question. This is most effectively done when the analyst connects to the customer's computer via remote control and conducts a show-and-tell session, but it can also work with the analyst just describing to the customer how to do it. To introduce the knowledge base, the analyst might say, "I bet that answer is in the knowledge base. Have you ever accessed it? It's a great tool, and I'd like to show it to you."

• Some internal support centers publish their cost per contact to the employees as an incentive to use web self-service before contacting the support center. This approach works best in organizations in which cost reduction is a corporate virtue.

• If you can identify who visits the web site, recognize the most-frequent users with a monthly listing in the corporate newsletter. Interview them to get testimonials on why they like to use it. Send them a certificate of recognition for being a top user of the month. Post their pictures and testimonials on the support web site. If practical, invite them to a party in the support center exclusively for frequent users.

• Recognize the most frequent contributors to the support forums in a similar manner to the one described for frequent users of the web site.

Best Practices – Support Web Site

1. The support center has a web site that includes some or all of these features:
   • Knowledge base and FAQs
   • Web-based support request entry
   • Product and documentation downloads
   • Forums

## CHAPTER NINE

Metrics and Reporting

"WHAT YOU CAN'T MEASURE, you can't manage" is an old management axiom that rings true in today's do-more-with-less environment. Metrics, or measurements, provide the data to manage the day-to-day operations of the support center. It is imperative that support center managers know how to measure both their agents' and the team's performance, and have the tools to do so. In this unit, we will study the commonly used metrics in spectacular support centers.

One challenge that most support centers face is integrating the statistics received from many sources, such as the service management system, the telephone-based automatic call distribution system, a knowledge base, and quality assurance methods such as customer satisfaction surveys and analyst monitoring processes. Chasing data can be a time-consuming activity. Many new tools are being consolidated on a single database platform, which lessens this challenge.

What intimidates many smaller support centers about reporting is the time commitment involved in creating the reports. Reporting is foundational to managing a spectacular support center, and the support manager needs to find clever ways to ensure that reporting is done regularly and in a timely manner. A manager might delegate reporting responsibilities to an analyst who is well informed about the support center tools and can automate as much as possible in the reporting process. If this person is also skilled with spreadsheets, much integration can be done to make the reports automatically pull data from the proper sources. Automate as much as your tools will let you. It is very satisfying to find a support center report in your in-box every morning. Lastly, simplify the following reports to serve your needs. Do what you must to ensure that reporting is done religiously.

Reporting is foundational to managing a spectacular support center.

Let us look at metrics commonly used in support centers. Starting on this page is a table of metrics, along with definitions, sources, benefits and comments. Each support center should examine this list and decide which metrics or key performance indicators (KPIs) are important for its unique environment.

Common Support Center Metrics

Metric	Definition	Source	Applicable to team or to analyst?	Benefits/comments
Number of support requests handled	The number of support requests touched by an analyst or a team.	The service management system	Both	Some support centers use this as a productivity measure, but it is difficult to compare results from analysts who perform dissimilar duties. Consideration for vacation, sick days and scheduled time on the phones is needed to do comparisons.
Number of support requests resolved	The total number of support requests resolved by an analyst or a team.	The service management system	Both	

Common Support Center Metrics – continued

Metric	Definition	Source	Applicable to team or to analyst	Benefits/comments
First con-tact reso-lutin rate (FCR)	The percentage of sup-port requests resolved on first contact.	The serv-ice man-agement system	Both	This is both an efficiency measure and an effectiveness measure. It is a leading indica-tor of customer satisfaction because customers want their support requests resolved immediately. Also important to the support center because high FCR saves money. Beware of putting too much focus on this metric without balancing it with re-open rates. Analysts have a tendency to "solve" problems that may not really be solved just to game this metric.
Re-open Rate	The percentage of sup-port requests that were coded as resolved but were re-opened within 3 (or X) busi-ness days.		Both	This metric balances FCR.
First-level resolution rate	The percentage of sup-port requests resolved at first-level without escalation outside of the support center.	The serv-ice man-agement system	Team	This is an efficiency measure for the support center. It is less expensive to solve support requests in the support center than solving them at third-level.
Service level	The percentage of contacts responded to within X seconds. For example, 85 percent of calls within 30 sec-onds.	ACD	Team	A responsiveness measure and a leading indicator of customer satisfaction. Customers have little tolerance for waiting on hold. Larger support centers tend to track this metric rather than average speed of answer, below. This metric can be applied to incoming calls or electronic requests but should be separately tracked for each contact media.
Average speed of answer (ASA)	On average, how quick-ly the support center responds to incoming contacts.	ACD	Team	Another way of measuring response. Because averages have a tendency to hide real performance, this may be less accurate a measure than service level. This metric can be applied to incoming calls or electronic

Common Support Center Metrics – continued

Metric	Definition	Source	Applicable to team or to analyst?	Benefits/comments
				requests but is separately tracked for each contact media.
Abandon rate	Percentage of total calls offered that were abandoned (the customer hung up) before being connected with an analyst.	ACD	Team	Most ACDs allow you to set thresholds for tracking abandon rate. Most support centers set their threshold to the time it takes a customer to navigate through the IVR greeting and menu. In the case of outage messages posted as the IVR greeting, the number of abandons before the threshold contributes to a "calls avoided" metric that reflects the support center's self-service effectiveness.
Percent of electronic requests responded to within X hours	Percent of electronic support requests that receive a response from an analyst within 4 hours of receipt of the request.	Service management system	Both	Because they are asynchronous forms of communication, electronic request handling can be more efficient than phone service. To encourage customers to use this media, response time should be within 4 hours.
Average handle time	The average talk time plus the average after-call work time. After-call work time is the time the analyst spends entering information into the service management system and any time spent researching the support request.	ACD and the service management system	Both	This metric is an important input into staffing calculations. Most service management systems have a time tracking feature that allows them to track the time the analyst spent resolving support requests.
Analyst availability	Of the scheduled on-phone time, the percentage of time the analyst was either handling a call or waiting for the next call. The opposite metric, the unavailable rate, could also be tracked. Unavailable rate is the percentage of the analyst's scheduled phone	ACD	Analyst	Used as a productivity measure for individuals and is a useful comparison metric across all positions and responsibilities within the support center.

Common Support Center Metrics – continued

Metric	Definition	Source	Applicable to team or to analyst?	Benefits/comments
	time that the analyst was in unavailable status on the ACD.			
Customer satisfaction	The customer's ratings of the service provided. Surveys commonly use a 1-5, 1-7 or 1-10 rating scale. Customer satisfaction is reported as top box score (percentage of scores that represent very satisfied or better ratings) and satisfaction score (percentage of scores that represent satisfied or better ratings).	The service management system	Both	Can be reported as an average or a percentage. Because averages have a tendency to hide real performance, many support centers opt to report satisfaction in percentages of ratings, e.g.: 90% top box score.
SLA target attainment	The percentage of support requests that were responded to and resolved within SLA guidelines.	The service management system	Team	This is a measure of the entire organization's responsiveness to the customer. The support center is dependent on its escalation groups to respond according to OLA and SLA guidelines. The support center is responsible for reporting these metrics.
Service monitoring scores	Scores given during observation of analysts while they interact with customers. This could also include ticket monitoring, in which the support request record is evaluated for completeness, accuracy and problem-solving methodology. Generally, an evaluation form is used to create an overall score for the interaction. Scores are tabulated for each analyst and summarized in periodic reporting.	Service monitoring database (could be a spreadsheet tool)	Analyst	This is the internal measure of quality service. Performing service monitoring is a commitment of time on the part of managers, but is necessary to ensure consistent, high quality service. Affords opportunities for positive coaching of analysts and disciplines managers to take the time to provide ongoing feedback to analysts.

Common Support Center Metrics – continued

Metric	Definition	Source	Applicable to team or to analyst?	Benefits/comments
Knowledge solution-s created	The number of knowledge solutions created or edited.	Knowledge base	Typically analysts but could be team also	Many support centers create a monthly or quarterly goal for solutions created or edited per analyst.
Solution quality rating	The percentage of criteria on the solution quality review form that was met.	Solution quality review database or spreadsheets	Both	A part of the knowledge management process is to review the solution creation quality.
Cost per contact	The total cost of support divided by the number of contacts received. Total cost comes from the support center budget and includes salaries, benefits, training plus facilities, hardware/software costs and any other costs that can be accrued to the support center.	ACD, service management system and financials	Team	Financial metrics are usually the last to be tracked and reported in a support center's maturation. Their presence indicates a mature support center.
Cost per support request	The total cost of support divided by the number of support requests handled.	The service management system and financial	Team	Number of contacts and number of support requests will generally not be the same number, as many contacts may be received for one support request.
Cost per customer	The total cost of support divided by the total number of customers.	The service management system and financials	Team	Can be used to project costs as the number of customers increase. Can also be used for charge-back calculations for internal support centers.
Backlog of open support requests	The total number of open support requests. This is usually reported by the group that owns the support request.	The service management system	Both	Typically, an internal support center will have few open support requests. Support centers that provide complex support tend to retain ownership of support requests longer, and therefore a backlog will be more of a support request.

Common Support Center Metrics – continued

Metric	Definition	Source	Applicable to team or to analyst?	Benefits/comments
Number of solutions linked	Number of knowledge base solutions used by the analysts to solve support requests.	Knowledge base and service management system	Both	This is used as an effectiveness measure of the knowledge base. It can also identify coaching opportunities for those analysts who do not access the knowledge base and are seeking answers from second-level support instead.
Employee satisfaction rate	The percentage of employees who are satisfied or better as measured by an internal employee satisfaction survey.	Survey tool	Team	Even small support centers can conduct an employee satisfaction survey once a year.
Average employee tenure	Total tenure of the support center divided by the number of analysts.	Human resources records	Team	A measure of employee satisfaction in which higher is better.
Employee retention rate	Percentage of analysts who remain with the support center. Calculation: # of analysts still employed at period end divided by (# of analysts at period start plus new positions created).	Human resources records	Team	A measure of employee satisfaction.
Time to analyst proficiency	For new hires, the time it takes to be able to handle customer request independently.	Training records	Team	Reducing time to proficiency saves time and money for the support center.
Training hours completed	Hours of training completed by support center employees.	Training records	Team	This is a measure of the organization's commitment to continuous learning.
Calls avoided	Number of successful self-service events recorded. Can also be expressed as a percentage of the total potential contacts received. Calculation: # of self-service events divided by (total contacts plus # of self-service events).	Web site and knowledge base	Team	This can be determined by summing all the product/documentation downloads completed (customers would otherwise have to call for this information) and the number of times that the knowledge base solved the customer's support request. This can be determined through surveys of web users.

Common Support Center Metrics – continued

Metric	Definition	Source	Applicable to team or to analyst?	Benefits/comments
Main-tenance renewal rate	The percentage of cus-tomers who renewed their maintenance/sup-port contract during the period. Calculation: # of customers who renewed divided by number of customers eligible for renewal.	Accoun-ting records	Team	A customer loyalty measure.

Common Support Center Reports

There are three periodic reports that a support center typically runs to manage its operations and several reports that the support center runs to show SLA compliance. The support center reports are:

1. Support center daily report
2. Analyst monthly scorecard
3. Support center balanced scorecard

Each of these reports draws information from a variety of sources, including the service management system, as we noted previously. Larger support centers have access to powerful data warehousing and integrated reporting systems, but typically small to mid-sized support centers do not have such resources. Creating the integrated reports in a spreadsheet works well for most support centers. Some groups are able to link spreadsheet reports and auto-mate some of the data entry work needed to amalgamate the data from separate sources.

Support Center Daily Report

The first report is the daily report. As its name implies, it is run every morning and displays the previous day's activities. Many sup-port center managers hold a standing meeting with their teams or supervisors every morning to review the previous day's performance. This daily review keeps the entire team focused on the accomplishments of the group by displaying the key performance indicators that are important in your environment. Even in a small support center, the

Many support center managers hold a standing meeting with their teams or supervisors every morning.

manager should be running daily reports to review the previous day's activities and performance.

On page 130 is an example of a daily report.

Notice that this report shows the aging of the backlog of open tickets by escalation group. Escalation groups are the internal groups that receive escalations from the support center. Although it is not the responsibility of the support center to resolve escalated support requests, it is the duty of the support center to report to upper management the aging of open support requests. Because backlogs tend to get out of hand quickly, it is important to monitor the backlog daily. If the support manager notices an upward trend in any backlog, it is her duty to notify upper management of the potential to miss SLA deadlines.

Analyst Monthly Scorecard

Spectacular support centers compile a monthly report of metrics for each analyst. Metrics included in this report are those important to measure the productivity and contribution of each analyst. If you refer to the table of metrics displayed earlier in this chapter, you will find a description of each of the measurements included in the following report template.

Many smaller support centers have a negative reaction to measuring and displaying individual metrics, thinking that it creates an atmosphere of distrust or a "sweatshop" environment. This may

Support Center Daily Report

Metric	Target	Actual
		(date)
Average speed of answer	15 seconds	
Service Level	85% within 30	
# of calls offered		
# of calls answered		
Abandon rate	<5%	
Average handle time	<8 minutes	
# calls per analyst	>20	
# issues created		
# issues closed		
# issues resolved on first contact		
First contact resolution rate	80%	
Incoming emails		
Response within 4 hours	100%	
Response within 8 hours	0%	
Response within >8 hours	0%	
Aging	**Target**	**Actual**
Backlog aging – All support requests:		
Open support requests		
Open support requests <5 days old		
Open support requests between 5 & 10 days old		
Open support requests >10 days old		
Backlog – escalation group 1:		
Open support requests		
Open support requests <5 days old		
Open support requests between 5 & 10 days old		
Open support requests >10 days old		
Backlog – escalation group 2:		
Open support requests		
Open support requests <5 days old		
Open support requests between 5 & 10 days old		
Open support requests >days old		

have been true in the early days of the support center, but most analysts now expect to be evaluated according to measurable elements.

If you consider that most people want to do a good job, analyst metrics are a means to demonstrate the quality and productivity of the good analysts. The only analysts who should resent metrics are those who are not pulling their weight.

Analyst metrics are a means to demonstrate the quality and productivity of the good analysts.

In addition to publishing a report on each analyst's performance, support centers often create a score for each analyst, using a rating that combines the results from all the metrics. One way to attach a numeric rating to a metric is to create a 4-point scale that uses the mean (average) of all analysts' scores for that metric, plus 1 standard deviation and minus 1 standard deviation from the mean. The advantage of this is that the group average becomes the basis for all ratings, not an arbitrarily set number. This is most helpful in environments in which metric values may vary from month to month. Here is an example of that type of scoring:

Scoring Schema Using Mean and Standard Deviation of a Metric

	Numeric score	Example for AHT
	4 = scores >= A	
A = Mean plus 1 standard deviation	3 = scores between A and B	A = 9.3 minutes
B = Mean (average) of all scores:	2 = scores between B and C	B = Mean = 8.2 minutes Std dev = 1.1 minutes
C = Mean minus 1 standard deviation		C = 7.1 minutes
	1 = scores <= C	

Another way to attach scores to metrics is to assign points for each metric on the scorecard. The example on page 132 is for a service monitoring scoring scheme that uses a 5-point (0-4) scale.

A roll-up of each analyst's monthly scores should be incorporated into that individual's annual performance evaluation. Each organization's performance evaluation forms are different, but there

Scoring Schema Using Defined Levels

Numeric score:	Quality score:
4	93% and above
3	Between 87% and 92.9%
2	Between 80% and 86.9%
1	Between 72% and 79.9%
0	Below 71.9%

should be some section or sections of the standard form that correspond to the metrics used in the analyst's monthly report. Support managers should work with their human resources representative to integrate the analyst's metrics into the annual performance evaluation process.

The following two pages show examples of an analyst scorecard.

Note in Example 1 that the team average is included for each metric, but the report only displays the actual achievements of one analyst. In this way, the analyst sees his performance in relation to the team average. Some support centers display the team's range of actual values instead of or in addition to the average. Goals are set for most of the metrics. Some support centers may wish to report the support requests handled and support requests resolved by hour only because the number of hours of phone time per day varies among analysts, therefore the hourly comparison is the only fair one.

This approach is the recommended one for newer support centers or centers in which turnover is high.

Example 2 of an analyst monthly scorecard is for the brave only.

In this report, all analysts in the support center are listed on the left side of the report so that everyone in the support center sees all the metrics. In some mature support centers, the analysts are so accustomed to looking at metrics that they want to know exactly where they stand among their peers each month. This is

Analyst Monthly Scorecard – Example 1
Date

Metric	Work Habits		Quality			Metrics						
	Days worked	Tardies	Customer satisfaction score (top box)	Service monitoring score	Kb solution quality score	Issues handled	Any issues handled per day	Issues resolved	AHT	% First-level resolution	% respond	% kb re-use
Goal	65%		>80%	>90%	>90%				?	?	<10%	25%
Team Aver.												
Month 1												
Month 2												
Month 3												
Month 4												
Month 5												
Month 6												
Month 7												
Month 8												
Month 9												
Month 10												
Month 11												
Month 12												

Analyst Monthly Scorecard – Example 2

Date

Metric	Work Habits		Quality			Metrics							
	Days worked	Tardies	Customer satisfaction score (top box)	Service monitoring score	Kb solution quality score	Issues handled	Any issues handled per day	Issues resolved	AHT	% first level resolution	% respond	% kb re-use
Goal	65%		>80%	>90%	>90%				?	?	<10%	25%
Team Aver.												
Analyst 1												
Analyst 2												
Analyst 3												
Analyst 4												
Analyst 5												
Analyst 6												
Analyst 7												
Analyst 8												
Analyst 9												
Analyst 10												
Analyst 11												
Analyst 12												

recommended only for mature centers in which the fear of metrics is ancient history in the minds of the support analysts

Support Center Balanced Scorecard

Just as the analysts receive a report of their performance monthly, so should the support center as a whole track its performance. Incorporating all performance indicators into an overall score for the group helps executives see immediately if the group is over- or under-performing to their goals.

The balanced scorecard approach to reporting performance has taken hold in the support center industry over the past several years. Robert Kaplan and David Norton first popularized the balanced scorecard[9] in 1996. Their premise was that traditional finance-based metrics were no longer adequate to judge the performance of any organization and that a more balanced view was indicated. The balanced scorecard approach espouses that four perspectives be used to create a more unified view of the organization's performance. The four perspectives in Kaplan and Norton's model are financial, customer, internal/business processes and learning/growth.

> **The balanced scorecard approach to reporting performance has taken hold in the support center industry.**

Many support center associations, such as Service Strategies[10] and HDI[11], have taken the balanced scorecard and modified it to use different perspectives that reflect the support center environment.

9 Robert S. Kaplan and David P. Norton, The Balanced Scorecard: Translating Strategy Into Action (Boston: Harvard Business School Press, 1996)

10 Service Strategies Corporation, "Certified Support Manager: Student Course Book," 2004, www.servicestrategies.com

11 Robert S. Last (editor), The Metrics Reference Guide: A Reference Guide to the Balanced Scorecard Service Model (Colorado Springs, CO: HDI, 2005)

HDI recommends these perspectives: customer satisfaction, employee satisfaction, costs/productivity and organizational maturity. As the name implies, the balanced scorecard provides a balanced view of the achievements of an organization. The following monthly report reflects HDI's a balanced scorecard approach to measuring the effectiveness of the support center.

Please refer to the matrix of metrics, preceding, and their definitions for an explanation of each line item in this report. In your support center, you may wish to streamline the number of metrics

Support Center Balanced Scorecard

Month of (date)				
	Goal:	Weight:	Actual for month:	Weighted score:
Customer satisfaction measure:				
Customer satisfaction rating (top box)	90%	8	92%	8
Service level within 30 seconds (phones)	85%	5	84%	5
SLA target attainment	90%	4	85%	4
First contact resolution rate	80%	3	81%	3
Percent of electronic support requests responded within 4 hours	85%	3	75%	3
Maintenance renewal rate	90%	3	91%	3
Abandon rate	5%	2	7%	1
Re-opened rate	10%	2	7%	3
Customer satisfaction performance		30		29
Employee satisfaction measure:				
Employee satisfaction eating	90%	10	82%	9
Employee average tenure	2	7	2.2	8
Employee retention rate	85%	8	79%	7
Employee satisfaction performance:		25		24
Productivity/financial measure:				
Cost per contact	$25	7	$27.53	6
Average handle time in minutes	8.2	6	8.9	5
Backing of unresolved support requests	100	6	115	5
Calls avoidance sate	15%	6	9%	4
Productivity/financial performance:		25		20
Organizational maturity:				
Time to analyst proficiency (in weeks)	8	7	9	6
Training hours completed	75	7	50	5
Solution quality rating	90%	6	85%	6
Organizational maturity performance:		20		16
Target support index:				
Actual support index:		100		91

used in each perspective to simplify the scorecard.

In this balanced scorecard, a support index has been created of the weighted elements in each perspective. Each of the four perspectives has been given an overall weight. In this example, the customer satisfaction perspective is weighted most heavily. If the support center were performing to expectations, the actual support index would be 100 or greater. In this example, the support center index is 90, indicating that the support center is not achieving its goals in the metrics listed in the report. With this scorecard, the manager can look back at each section to determine which are dragging down the score. In the previous example, the scores for both productivity/financial measures and organizational maturity are well below expectations. The manager would drill down farther to discover that none of the metrics in those sections achieved the target, calling for the implementation of an improvement plan for the support center.

As discussed, financial measures are extremely difficult for some smaller support centers to calculate. In these cases, the support center should simply omit the financial metrics and only include the productivity ones.

Whether the smaller support center chooses to follow the balanced scorecard model or create a simpler report, every support center should create monthly reports on its overall performance and deliver them to the support center and to executive management, with an explanation of what the metrics mean, if necessary. It is true that many upper managers do not understand the metrics common in the support center industry, so a commentary or interpretation of the reports sent up the organizational chart would enable better understanding of the support center's achievements.

Service Level Agreement Compliance

We discussed previously how best practices dictate that the support center assume cradle-to-grave ownership of all support requests. This means that the support center must be responsible for creating and producing SLA compliance reports that display the response and resolution performance of each escalation group.

The SLA compliance reports are run either weekly or monthly and are presented at a managerial meeting in which all escalation groups participate. It is imperative that in attendance is a high-ranking manager who is positioned at a point in the organizational chart where all the escalation groups converge. This manager must meet periodically with all of his or her managers to enforce SLA compliance. Ideally, each escalation group's performance should be evaluated on its ability to meet SLA targets.

On page 139 is an example of an SLA compliance report.

Other Reports

There are other reports that a support center manager might wish to run on an ongoing basis.

In order to identify training opportunities for the center, a report on the most frequently asked question types should be run for the support requests received at second-level. The report from the second-level queue will identify training needs for individual analysts.

Another report is the most frequent callers list and the nature of those calls. In both internal and external support centers, this can

The SLA compliance reports are run either weekly or monthly.

identify opportunities to suggest additional training for customers. Reports may be run on number of calls received, or on time taken to support individual departments or customer accounts. In an internal support center, this may be used for charge-back purposes.

SLA Response and Resolve Compliance
for XYZ Support Department
Goal = 96% compliance with SLA targets

	Priority 1			Priority 2			Priority 3			Priority 4			Priority 5			Overall Score
	# of P1 issues	P1 expense time - actual	P1 resolve time - actual	# of P2 issues	P2 resolve time - actual	P2 resolve time - aactual	# of P3 issues	P3 resolve time - actual	P3 resolve time - actual	# of P4 issues	P4 resolve time - actual	P4 resolve time - actual	# of P5 issues	P5 resolve time - actual	P5 resolve time - actual	Average of all scores
Goal:	N/A	15 min.	2 hrs.	N/A	30 min.	8 hrs.	N/A	4 hrs.	24 hrs.	N/A	8 hrs.	48 hrs.	N/A	N/A	As scheduled	
Months:																
Month 1		95%	93%		97%	98%		94%	96%		96%	98%			95%	96%
Month 2		94%	95%		94%	96%		97%	94%		95%	93%			93%	95%
Month 3		92%	94%		97%	96%		95%	95%		98%	92%			96%	95%
etc.																

Many external support centers run reports on the number of times a customer has called during the year and include that report in the customer's support contract renewal notice.

Best Practices – Metrics and Reporting

1. Even small support centers should commit to producing performance reports on a regular basis. What you cannot measure, you cannot manage.

2. Each support center should decide what its key performance indicators are. They are different for each group, depending on the needs of the larger organization, the customers and the support analysts.

3. The support center should run a daily report to check on the previous day's performance of the support center.

4. Analyst monthly scorecards should be run to tell analysts and managers how they are doing in relation to the team. The monthly scorecard results should flow into the analyst's annual performance review.

5. Monthly reports on the support center's overall performance are important.

6. Service level agreement and aging reports display the backlog of cases that have been escalated and the response time to them.

## CHAPTER TEN

Quality Assurance

IN A SUPPORT CENTER, there are two aspects of quality assurance: gathering customer feedback through surveys and other methods, and service monitoring, which is a direct inspection by the manager of a random sample of service interactions. The combination of these two sources of data gives a complete picture of the quality of the support center's product, which is service delivery. This is why we include both the customer survey scores and service monitoring scores on an analyst's monthly scorecard.

We will first look at customer surveying and feedback, then discuss the service monitoring process.

Customer Surveying and Feedback

Ultimately, the most important metric is the measurement of your customer's satisfaction with your service. Industry best practices dictate that every center should be regularly soliciting feedback from customers via surveys. In addition, most support centers find that regularly soliciting customer feedback provides information that can be used to improve service delivery. Customers can be the best source of suggestions for process and quality improvements.

Customer Satisfaction Process Structure

How you structure the process for soliciting survey data affects the outcomes you realize. There are several ways to implement the survey process to conform to industry best practices. In general, support centers use two types of surveys to gather customer feedback: an event survey and an annual survey.

Event Surveys

Event surveys are sent soon after a service event is completed or a support request is resolved. The intent of this survey is to gather feedback on the specific event, and even the specific analyst. Many

The intent of this survey is to gather feedback on the specific event.

support centers wait two or three days after the support request is closed before emailing a survey, to make sure that the support request is not re-opened and that the survey response is gathered on a resolved support request. However, be sure to send the survey relatively quickly so the customer does not forget what happened during the interaction. I recently received a survey from the airline I often use regarding a flight I took three weeks ago. I travel so often that I could not even remember that particular flight. In addition, there was no opportunity to offer comments even though it was a long questionnaire that took about 12 minutes to complete. I would have used a comments field to explain that I no longer remembered the flight.

Some support centers are opting to choose after-call IVR-based event surveys, in which the caller is transferred to the survey tool at the end of the phone call. This media, which ensures that the customer remembers the interaction, is found to be highly accurate.

A best practice is to exclude customers who have responded to an event survey within the last 30-45 days. This practice ensures that customers are not over-surveyed and can help boost response rates to the survey. Many service management systems generate surveys automatically and can enable this exclusion.

Event surveys should be brief and take customers no more than five minutes to complete unless they want to provide comments. Comments should be solicited at least once in the survey instrument, but many companies offer a comment field after each question in order to gather specific feedback. It is as important to categorize and report on comments as it is to calculate the numeric scores. Collating comments, unfortunately, takes more time and is more labor-intensive than numeric scores, which are usually calculated and reported automatically. Because comments may contain valuable suggestions for improving your operations, it is worth the extra effort to record, categorize and report them. By the way, it is possible that a customer gives high marks on the rated elements of the survey but appears unhappy in the comments field. A good support manager would contact the customer as if the survey were a poorly rated one.

Comments should be solicited at least once in the survey instrument.

To categorize comments, a support manager or survey administrator must read each survey, understand the comments offered, and either assign a pre-defined category or create a new category. For example, the comment received from the customer might be, "We tried many things that seemed to solve the problem at first, but now the same problem is happening again." The manager would categorize this comment as "not solved" and would follow up with the customer. Reporting the number of comments received under each category reveals important information.

You might report comment categories like this:

	Negative comments:	Response time	Not solved	Profes- sionalism	Product defect	User interface	Positive comments:	Profes- sionalism	Response time
Jan 1		13	2	0	5	7		6	0
Jan 8		7	5	1	7	8		5	1
Jan 15		6	3	1	8	7		3	2
Etc.									
Totals:		26	10	2	2	22		14	3

A manager might interpret this report as indicating the following:

- Response time was an issue during the busy week of January 1 but decreased as the month progressed. This is something to keep an eye on.
- Product defects received the second highest number of negative comments. Further investigation is warranted.
- Analyst professionalism was the most-common positive comment received. The support team deserves kudos!

A support center should devise a process to respond to low-rated surveys. Some service management systems can notify a manager upon receipt of a poor score, but smaller support centers must monitor this manually. Typically, the manager or supervisor of the analyst involved calls the customer to first apologize for the poor service, then works to resolve the issue. The manager may delegate technical troubleshooting to a senior analyst but should retain ownership of the customer's satisfaction. If the issue had to do with the analyst's service skills or troubleshooting skills, the manager may need to coach the analyst on those deficiencies. See Chapter Twelve: Team Management for help with coaching skills.

Many support centers include the results of the event survey in the analyst's monthly scorecard, as previously shown. It makes sense that if the best measure of the effectiveness of both the support center and the analyst is customer satisfaction, then that metric should be included in the scorecards for both. Especially for smaller support centers, it may be a challenge to receive enough survey results on each analyst to be statistically meaningful. Some support centers combat this by providing incentives for customers to participate in the survey. The incentive could be as simple as entering the customer's name into a monthly drawing for a small gift certificate, company t-shirt, hat or other paraphernalia. Other ways to encourage participation is to advertise survey results and what the support center has done in response to the feedback gathered, and to send the surveys out over the name of an executive, such as the CIO or CEO.

Even with these incentives, the smaller support center may not receive enough feedback on each analyst to include satisfaction scores in their monthly scorecard. If the sample size is too small, one poorly rated survey could adversely skew an otherwise reliable analyst's score. There are mathematical ways to calculate the confidence level of the survey data received, but a manager in a small support center can look at the data and intuitively check to see if the outcome seems in line with the analyst's performance patterns. One way to compensate for too few event surveys for an individual analyst is to track monthly but report semi-annually or yearly each individual analyst's satisfaction scores. Reporting for a longer time allows more survey data to accumulate. Alternatively, the manager might choose to use an overall team score instead of individual scores as a performance indicator.

The smaller support center may not receive enough feedback on each analyst to include satisfaction scores in their monthly scorecard.

Some support centers feel that the customer satisfaction rating is the most important metric of all, and they create incentives and rewards on this metric alone. In these centers, other individual metrics such as first contact resolution rate are considered hygienic only and might be classified as "meets expectations" (within guidelines) or "does not meet expectations." Any analyst who does not meet expectations is coached. This generally works best in mature support centers, small or large, in which good habits are already established, all analysts pull their own weight and management is strong.

The wording and format of the survey questions should be given careful thought. An overall satisfaction question such as, "How would you rate your overall satisfaction with this service event?" should always be included. In addition, consider creating questions concerning elements of the interaction on which you would like to gather feedback. Typically, those elements include response time, resolution time, resolution quality, the analyst's technical ability and the analyst's professional behavior. You may want to add or subtract questions according to your needs. For example, you may be concerned about response time to calls or electronic support requests at your support center. In that case, definitely include a question about that support request.

A best practice is to test your survey on a small group of customers and get their feedback on the survey instrument itself. Ask the participants if the questions were worded clearly, how long it took to complete the survey (remember the five-minute rule) and if there was any important service aspect that was omitted from the survey. You could facilitate this feedback session at a users' conference, via a conference call or in person with each tester.

Event Survey – Sample Instruments

Here are two examples of event survey instruments to use as templates for designing your event survey.

The first survey example comes from Fred Van Bennekom of

Great Brook Consulting. His book, *Customer Surveying: A Guidebook for Service Managers*, is a good resource for the support industry.[12] It is available at www.greatbrook.com. Notice that the invitation to this survey includes an incentive to participate.

Event Survey – Example 1

Thank you for agreeing to provide us feedback on your last service event with us, incident <4376> regarding a <printer problem>. Your feedback will help us ensure you consistently receive a high level of service. As a token of our thanks, we will enter your name in a monthly drawing for a <dollar amount> gift certificate to <vendor>.

Below you will find five brief descriptions of aspects of our service delivery. For each one please indicate how satisfied you were with each by circling the appropriate number on the 1 to 5 scale provided, where 5 represents extremely satisfied and 1 represents extremely dissatisfied. Click on the submit button when complete.

	Extremely satisfied	Neutral	Extremely dissatisfied
1. Once service delivery began, the time required to resolve your problem.	5	4 3	2 1
2. The ability to transfer issues between service agents without having to repeat the history of the problem.	5	4 3	2 1
3. The professional conduct of the service agent.	5	4 3	2 1
4. The service agent's technical knowledge.	5	4 3	2 1
5. The overall quality of the service transaction.	5	4 3	2 1

6. Comments:

The next example has slightly different questions and format.

---

[12] *Fred Van Bennekom, Ph.D., Customer Surveying: A Guidebook for Service Managers (Bolton, MA:Customer Service Press, 2002) Used with permission.*

Event Survey – Example 2

1. Overall, how would you rate the service you receive from the support center?

    5. Very satisfied

    4. Satisfied

    3. Neither satisfied nor dissatisfied

    2. Dissatisfied

    1. Extremely dissatisfied

2. Please indicate your level of satisfaction with the support center on the following attributes:

    a. Professionalism

        5. Very satisfied

        4. Satisfied

        3. Neither satisfied nor dissatisfied

        2. Dissatisfied

        1. Extremely dissatisfied

    b. Knowledgeable

        5. Very satisfied

        4. Satisfied

        3. Neither satisfied nor dissatisfied

        2. Dissatisfied

        1. Extremely dissatisfied

    c. Quality of the resolution

        5. Very satisfied

        4. Satisfied

        3. Neither satisfied nor dissatisfied

        2. Dissatisfied

        1. Extremely dissatisfied

    d. Speed to resolve your problem

        5. Very satisfied

        4. Satisfied

        3. Neither satisfied nor dissatisfied

        2. Dissatisfied

        1. Extremely dissatisfied

e. Speed of response to your phone call or email

    5. Very satisfied

    4. Satisfied

    3. Neither satisfied nor dissatisfied

    2. Dissatisfied

    1. Extremely dissatisfied

3. Comments or suggestions for improving our services:

Periodic Surveys

Periodic surveys are generally longer surveys that are meant to gather feedback on the performance of all customer-facing service groups and the products the customers use. A best practice is to send the periodic survey to all customers once a year. However, in order to receive a continuous flow of information, some organizations split the customer base into four segments and send the periodic survey to a different segment each quarter.

A periodic survey might be organized into the following sections:

• Satisfaction with the products

• Satisfaction with the support center

• Satisfaction with sales (external support centers)

• Satisfaction with IT services (internal support center)

The support center's section should include a question that allows the customer to rate the overall satisfaction with the services provided by the support center. Keep in mind that the answers to questions will reflect the customer's satisfaction with the support center in general, not just one encounter. Of course, even an event survey has a tendency to measure the customer's satisfaction with all of his or her interactions with the company or IT organization. Both industry studies and my own experience demonstrate that customer dissatisfaction with the product generally colors or influences her rating of the support center.

If the support center is able to allocate funds to pay for customer incentives to participate in a survey, those funds should be prioritized for the periodic survey. Response rates to periodic surveys tend to be lower than event surveys, due to the survey's length and other factors. The allure of participating in a drawing for a free iPod or some other gift may entice more customers to participate in the survey. Some other ways to increase response rates to this survey are to send it via email over the name of a company executive, and to send reminder emails once or twice to those who have not responded. A response rate in the high teens (for example, 18 percent) is good for a periodic survey.

Web Support Surveys

Many support centers create a separate survey for those customers who access web-based self-service. It is important to receive feedback on the success of the support web site so the support center can improve self-service options and therefore entice more customers to use it. Some of the questions you might ask the customers are:

- How often do you access self-service on the web?
- Rate the ease of searching for and finding a solution.
- Rate the completeness of the knowledge on the self-service site.
- Did you resolve the problem solely using self-service?

The answer to the last question is especially important to support centers that are trying to quantify the benefit of their self-service web site. The tools available today to measure the effectiveness of web self-service are rudimentary at best, and many support centers use the feedback from the last question on this survey to extrapolate the number of users who were successful in using self-service. Support centers can estimate the self-service success rate and the call avoidance cost/benefit by quantifying the percentage of responses to the survey that indicate a resolution was found through the web site and applying that to the number of hits received on the web site that month.

Gathering Feedback in Person

Managing a smaller support center often provides the support team with more opportunities to meet with customers face-to-face, due to the relatively lower number of customers served than larger centers. Gathering direct customer feedback has a dual purpose: to be able to have a dialogue about the customer's perception of support, and to pay attention to the customer and show that you care. Attention to customers is the most potent way of demonstrating how important they are to you.

Ways to gather direct customer feedback for external support centers include:

- Create a customer advisory council that meets regularly to provide direction to the company. The group may meet via phone most times but face-to-face with company executives at least once yearly.
- Staff a booth at customer conferences with support analysts who offer on-the-spot technical support. Offer customers who visit the booth the opportunity to complete a special survey about their experience with customer support.
- Also at a customer conference, conduct a formal feedback session on customer support with your customers. Start with a presentation on what customer support has done for the customers recently, citing statistics that include response and resolution metrics as well as customer satisfaction and loyalty measures.
- Visit customers one-on-one to gather their feedback.
- Identify the top 10 most valuable customers to the company and assign an executive to each one. The executive is

responsible for contacting that customer quarterly to ask how things are going and to gather feedback.

The following ideas are for internal support centers to help them gather direct feedback:

- Create a customer advisory council that meets regularly to provide direction to the IT organization. The group may meet via phone most times but face-to-face with IT management once quarterly.

- Select a department in the company or a floor in the building to visit every week or month. Send a seasoned support analyst to walk the floor, ask employees if they are having any problems and note any feedback the customers offer. This is a wonderful way to provide proactive support, catch small problems before they balloon into larger ones and provide a face of the support center to the customers.

- Position analysts at a table in the cafeteria during lunchtimes. Provide them with support center brochures and special surveys to gather feedback on IT services and the support center. Do this periodically throughout the year.

- As support manager, personally visit local customers who give either high or low scores on the event survey. Call ahead and make an appointment, saying, "I'd like to personally review your satisfaction with the support center. I'm looking forward to an honest and constructive conversation." Go over the survey scores, asking after each question, "Is there something more about this element that I should know about?" If you receive negative feedback, be polite, curious and appreciative of the honest feedback. Vow to work to improve the situation with words like, "I really appreciate that you shared this with me. I will do my best to make this better for you. When I come back to visit in a year, I hope you'll tell me that things are much better."

When I was vice president of a software company, I traveled to a different city every other month to visit four customers a day. The purpose of the trip was specifically to gather customer feedback and to hear what was important to the customers. I would start the conversation by asking what my company was doing well for the customer and then ask what we could do better. I remember one or two tense conversations, but mostly my memories are of honest and open conversations in which I would gather vast amounts of helpful information regarding both our services and products. My follow-up activities consisted of writing thank-you notes to the customers I visited and creating summary reports of what I heard in order to share the information with product development and the executive team. Many of the improvements made in both product development and support developed from the feedback gathered in these fruitful conversations.

Service Monitoring Process

To ensure that quality standards are met, factories randomly inspect the quality of the product as it comes off the assembly line every day. Why shouldn't the support center also inspect the quality of its product, which is the service interaction? The old management adage says, "Inspect what you expect." If we do not inspect the service delivery product, how do we know if our analysts are delivering up to expectations? Even the smallest support center should have some form of quality assurance. With some key modifications to processes, smaller centers can attain or exceed the quality results of larger centers.

There are many benefits to establishing a service monitoring program for your analysts. Benefits include:

- Ensuring consistent and professional service.
- Enforcing customer service skills learned in training.

- Demonstrating the importance of customer service.
- Approximating and measuring your customers' satisfaction with your service.
- Improving morale by instituting standards for a quality interaction, recognizing those who meet or exceed expectations and coaching those who do not.

The goals of a quality program are to ensure consistent, high quality service, to recognize those analysts who are doing a great job and to identify opportunities for analyst training. Analyst scorecards or other departmental reports often include the results of the service monitoring evaluations along with other more tangible metrics such as number of calls handled, average handle time, first contact resolution rate and customer satisfaction scores.

The goals of a quality program are to ensure consistent, high quality service, to recognize those analysts who are doing a great job and to identify opportunities for analyst training.

A service monitoring program should be a positive step for your support center and it should be marketed to the analysts as such. Under no circumstances should it be portrayed as a punishment or disciplinary action. In every support center, there are three kinds of analysts: the stars or outstanding analysts, the average performers and the under-performing employees. A quality program allows the supervisor to identify the analysts who fit into each category and encourage each analyst to improve his performance through positive coaching and training opportunities.

The Process

It is important that the support center create a closed-loop process that ensures that service monitoring is conducted regularly and that the results are recorded and fed into other processes. That process can be depicted like this:

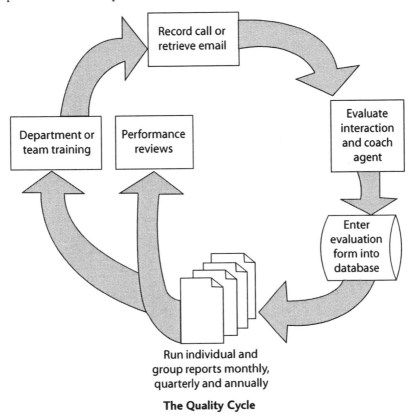

The Quality Cycle

The diagram and process description depicts the process to evaluate both electronic and telephone-based interactions. The same process can be used for both media.

Record Call or Retrieve Electronic Record

The process begins with recording or listening to a call or

retrieving the support request record in the service monitoring system. It is important for the supervisor to be able to listen to a recorded call, but it is beneficial for the analysts to hear their own calls. I once managed an analyst who had a loud phone voice. Although I mentioned to her that she need not speak so forcefully, it was not until she heard her voice on a recording that she realized she was shouting at the customer.

Many smaller support centers are at a disadvantage right away, as they may not have access to advanced audio recording of telephone calls. Additionally, some small support centers do not have a phone system that allows the supervisor to monitor calls remotely. If the support center has no monitoring capability, the supervisor must conduct phone monitoring side-by-side (see below) or the manager may opt to conduct only ticket monitoring (see note on page 159 on smaller center considerations). Please refer to Chapter Seven: Support Tools for a discussion on recording system options for smaller support centers.

Ways to Monitor

There are three ways to monitor the professionals within the contact center.

1. The supervisor remotely listens, records and evaluates a call, then sets up a coaching session for that analyst. During the coaching session, both the supervisor and analyst listen to the recorded call, review the strengths displayed during the call and talk about how the analyst can improve her skills. This approach is best when analysts are inexperienced, having performance problems or just learning the call evaluation form. The supervisor enters the evaluation results into a quality database.

2. Peer monitoring can be effective for newer analysts. In peer

monitoring, a senior member of the team is paired with a junior one, and the more experienced analyst evaluates a call taken by the junior member and vice versa. This is usually done sitting side-by-side. This method allows the junior member to learn best practices and gives the more experienced analyst a chance to mentor. Usually, peer evaluations are not entered into the quality database without a supervisor present to guard against skewing the ratings.

3. For experienced analysts, self-evaluation works well. In this instance, the supervisor and the analyst listen to the same call, either separately or together. They both rate the call and then discuss it. Many times, analysts evaluate themselves more harshly than the supervisor would. In this case, the supervisor will "soften" the rating and input the evaluation results into the quality database.

How often should analysts be monitored? Best practices indicate that managers should monitor new support analysts often, perhaps once a day for the first week then twice weekly for the next month. As an analyst becomes more experienced, the frequency can decline. Twice a month per analyst is a good rule of thumb, unless something suggests that a particular individual needs more attention. Some centers include several calls in the twice-monthly monitoring – that is an individual center's decision. Triggers to conduct monitoring on an analyst more often than twice monthly include:

- Receiving more than one poorly rated event survey for the analyst in the past quarter.
- Receiving a complaint from a customer about the analyst.
- Perceiving a trend of poor service-monitoring scores.

Finally, those analysts who have a proven record of providing outstanding customer service may be allowed to graduate to monthly monitoring sessions conducted through a self-evaluation as described on page 157.

Evaluate Interaction and Coach Analyst

The next step in the process is to evaluate the interaction and coach the analyst using an evaluation form. A sample evaluation form along with its legend, which is a lengthy description of each line item on the evaluation form, is found in Appendix A. Use this form as is, or customize it to the specifications of the support center. Coaching is discussed beginning on page 194.

Enter Evaluation Into Database

In larger support centers, the call recording tool may have an evaluation database built into it. Some smaller support centers have access to this functionality through newer, reasonably priced Voice over IP (VoIP) telephone systems. However, many support centers do not have access to this functionality.

In its simplest form, a database of evaluations could be a network directory in which the manager stores all the spreadsheets of completed evaluations. Alternatively, many support centers identify an analyst with technical proclivities to program a tool in Microsoft Access or another database. This tool presents an evaluation form to the manager and stores all completed evaluations. The advantage of this effort is that the programmer can create reports of the evaluation data. This functionality saves an enormous amount of time that would otherwise be spent doing manual data collection and reporting. Chapter Seven: Support Tools explores the benefits of a service monitoring tool and how to find a reasonably priced one.

Run Reports

Ideally, data from the service monitoring program feed into the analyst's monthly scorecard and ultimately into the annual performance review. Without a reporting capability, running reports may be a manual task of entering the averaged final scores of the monthly monitors into the analyst's monthly scorecard.

Department Training/Performance Reviews

If trending analysis is possible on the individual elements of the service monitoring evaluation, the manager can identify possible training needs by reviewing the reports. For example, if a significant number of monitors indicate a lack of troubleshooting skills, the manager would ask the training coordinator to develop and schedule a special training class on that subject. Individual training opportunities also can be identified through service monitoring. The manager or supervisor who conducts the monitoring usually identifies training opportunities as they monitor and coach individuals in their team.

A summary of the analyst's monthly scorecard, which includes service monitoring scores, should be included in some fashion in the analyst's performance review. Often, performance metrics are referenced in the performance review. You may need to speak with a human resources representative to plan how to incorporate the quality program

> **A summary of the analyst's monthly scorecard should be included in the analyst's performance review.**

scores into the analyst's annual performance reviews. That person will undoubtedly have ideas and opinions about where and how you can include the scores. Explain to the HR person that including the scores in the analyst's review adds teeth to the program and demonstrates its importance.

Considerations for Smaller Support Centers

Large support centers have elaborate processes, tools and teams of people that enable their quality assurance programs. In these centers, full-time employees are dedicated to monitoring the quality of the service. These employees listen to and evaluate calls, run reports and provide trending data on service monitoring to the support management team. They might also coordinate the customer feedback and surveying procedures.

For support centers that are small enough for the manager to hear most conversations while sitting at her desk, a full-blown service monitoring program is overkill. What is recommended for these centers is to conduct regular ticket monitoring rather than the complete service monitoring. Ticket monitoring involves randomly selecting support requests for each analyst on a regular basis and reviewing the documentation entered into the service management system. In this way, the manager can assess the troubleshooting skills and the analyst's compliance with standard operating procedures. The call evaluation form found later in this chapter can be abbreviated to use only the last section, titled ticket review. The ticket evaluation might include:

- Did the analyst enter the customer information correctly?
- Did the analyst properly verify the entitlement of the customer?
- Did the analyst categorize and prioritize the support request correctly?
- Did the analyst document the problem description accurately?
- Was the documentation free of spelling errors and easy to understand?
- Did the analyst document all resources checked (i.e.: knowledge base) and document troubleshooting steps taken?
- If the call was escalated, did the analyst collect all the relevant

data for effective escalation?

- Did the analyst link to the knowledge base correctly?
- Did the analyst correctly close the record?

You can reproduce these questions in a spreadsheet, using the format and layout of the call evaluation form. Present and discuss the form and your expectations with all the analysts. Each support center should set a goal of reviewing X tickets per analyst per month and coaching the analysts in one-on-one meetings at least once monthly.

In these small centers, if a manager hears a service interaction going poorly, she should immediately intervene and either talk to the analyst or conference in on the call. In this way, the manager is coaching the analysts on customer service skills in an ongoing manner.

How to Find Time for Service Monitoring

The number one reason that smaller support centers do not conduct service monitoring is lack of time. Managers of smaller centers have all the responsibilities of running a support center but have fewer people to delegate to. (Many smaller support center managers are able to delegate more than they think, however.) In addition, smaller support center managers often serve customers themselves, diverting their attention from managerial duties. In a small support center, the manager is constantly taking off one hat to put on another, in the sense of constantly assuming different roles during the day. However, quality is just as important in a smaller center as in a large one. If you do not inspect what you expect, you will not get the desired results.

Here are some ways to fit service monitoring into your schedule:

- Commit to it. Make quality assurance a priority. Delegate other tasks so you have time to do it. Include service monitoring scores on the analyst's monthly scorecard so you are accountable for the program.

- Modify the program to make it easier to perform. Do only ticket monitoring, as previously described. Alternatively, reduce the number of monitors you conduct each month or each quarter; for example, commit to formally monitoring your best analysts only twice a quarter.

- Incorporate the service monitoring program into your monthly one-on-one meetings with each analyst. Yes, you should be doing monthly one-on-one meetings with each analyst.

- Delegate the responsibility for performing monitoring to one of your best analysts or a senior analyst by creating a role of service monitoring specialist. Manage this person's activities by conducting a calibration session monthly with the specialist.

- Listen to recordings of calls during your commute to or from work. Find a way to convert the recordings to a format that you can play in the car (on an MP3 player, iPod, CD player or tape player). This can offload a time-consuming activity to a period of the day in which you are captive but able to listen.

How to Create a Service Monitoring Program

Implementing a service monitoring program is the mark of a maturing support center. There may be many reasons to embark on a service monitoring process. Perhaps there has been a difficult employee situation and you need to define metrics and performance standards for the group. Perhaps customers have complained about the quality of support they have received, and you need to implement programs to measure and improve service quality. Or perhaps you have added a number of new employees over the recent past and need to create standards for how all support analysts are going to treat the customers. Whatever the reason, implementing a service monitoring program is a best practice in the support industry. Here is how to create one:

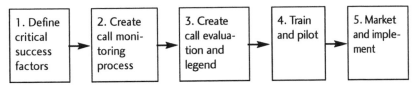

Creating the Service Monitoring Process

Step 1: Define Critical Success Factors

The first step in this project is to identify a task force, composed of analysts and managers in the support center, to work through this process. Together, they can identify goals and intended outcomes and assign tasks to individuals in order to achieve results. The task force needs to define success in this project. Together, the group must answer the following questions:

- Why are we doing this? What are our goals?
- What will success look like, or in other words, what outcomes do we want to see?
- How will we measure our success?
- What concerns or fears do we have?

Desired outcomes of quality programs are generally to improve quality of service. Success is best measured by the confluence of two metrics: the service monitoring scores generated through this program and the direct measurement of customer satisfaction through surveying methods, as discussed in the analyst monthly scorecard in Chapter Nine: Metrics and Reporting.

The task force should answer each of the questions above. It is important to discuss the concerns and fears each person may have because people often have prejudices about service monitoring that are based on past experiences or on negative rumors about programs. Make careful note of the fears so you can address them in your marketing program during rollout.

Clarifying objectives, expected results and metrics at this point will influence all subsequent work and will ensure understanding across the task force. Be sure to document your conclusions and share them with everyone on the task force, executive champions and any additional stakeholders to the process.

Step 2: Create and Document the Contact Monitoring Process

In this step, we need to answer the following questions:

- Who is going to perform service monitoring?
- How will we record calls and/or keystrokes? Do we need to purchase equipment?
- How often will we monitor the analysts? (See page 157 for recommendations for monitoring frequency.)
- How will service monitoring data feed into reporting and performance evaluations?
- How will we ensure that all supervisors are evaluating consistently?
- How will we recognize those analysts who provide outstanding service?

In a smaller support center, the manager or supervisor generally performs service monitoring. Recording calls is an important step in the service monitoring process. See Chapter Seven: Support Tools for advice on finding recording systems for smaller support centers.

If the service monitoring program is to have any impact, its results must be stored and reported. In Chapter Nine: Metrics and Reporting, we discussed the analyst monthly scorecard, which includes both customer satisfaction and service monitoring metrics. These metrics should also flow into the performance evaluation process.

A challenge for mid-sized support centers with more than one supervisor is ensuring that all service evaluations are consistently scored. One supervisor may interpret the requirements for a particular element on the evaluation differently than another, resulting in inconsistent scores across the teams. A best practice for mid-sized support centers is to conduct monthly calibration sessions, in which all the supervisors and the manager meet to listen to a recorded call and score the interaction. The group discusses the scores given each element and comes to consensus on what the correct rating is. This level of discipline is necessary if the support center is reporting service monitoring results on the analyst monthly scorecard.

In the section on Rewards and Recognition in Chapter Twelve: Team Management, there is a discussion on how to recognize analysts who have achieved excellent quality.

Lastly, create a document that outlines the service monitoring process. It is helpful to outline the tasks in a weekly, monthly and yearly format. If you agreed, for example, that each analyst should have two coaching sessions per month, your quality process outline might look like this:

Weekly:
- Record and evaluate calls for one-fourth of the analysts on the team.
- Prepare coaching for call(s) evaluated.
- Coach analysts.
- Record evaluations in spreadsheet (or database).

Monthly:
- Run summary reports.
- Incorporate quality scores into analyst and department scorecards.
- Conduct calibration session with supervisors and manager(s).

Yearly:
- Run yearly summary reports.

- Incorporate quality scores into analyst performance reviews.
- Review effectiveness of the service monitoring program.

Step 3: Create Call Evaluation Form, Legend and Analyst's Scorecard

It is easier for a group to react to a template than to create something new, so the following call evaluation template is offered on page 167 and in Appendix A as a starting point for discussion in this step.

Examine each line item on the template and decide if it is something important to your support center. Delete those that are not important and add elements that you think are important. For example, if your analysts do not need to replicate the problem, delete line 7 from the template. You also need to create a legend, or description, to accompany the call evaluation form. The legend defines in detail the behaviors expected of the analysts in each step of the call's structure. The legend can include suggested wordings for each question of the evaluation. The legend in Appendix A includes many phrases that have been proven to work well with customers and that are based on principals of good communication.

The next decision is how to score the evaluation form. Obvious choices are a graded system or a pass/fail system. A comprehensive legend allows a support center to use a pass/fail system because it defines in detail the expected behaviors for each element of the evaluation form. Although many support centers use a graded system such as a 1 to 5 score (similar to a customer satisfaction survey scoring system), a pass/fail system is undeniably simpler. However, there may be some aspects to your evaluation form that fit well with a numeric scoring system.

A comprehensive legend allows a support center to use a "yes-no" or "met-not met" grading system.

The template in this book shows a percentage score that

Call and Ticket Evaluation Form

Analyst:
Supervisor:
Meter number: (where to find the call recording, if applicable)
Date:

Call segment:	YES	NO	N/A
Greeting:			
1. Was standard greeting used?	YES		
Problem identification:			
2. Did the analyst actively listen to customer?		NO	
3. Did the analyst paraphrase and confirm the problem description?	YES		
4. Did the analyst ask appropriate questions to properly identify the problem?		NO	
Analysis:			
5. Did the analyst ask appropriate questions to explore conditions and troubleshoot?	YES		
6. Did the analyst effectively use his/her resources to research possible solutions?	YES		
7. Did the analyst replicate the customer's problem?	YES		
8. Did the analyst follow escalation guidelines and escalate when appropriate?			NA
Resolution:			
9. Did the analyst educate the customer on how to use the self-service knowledge base?		NO	
10. Did the analyst state the resolution plan in a clear manner?	YES		
11. Did the analyst walk the customer through the steps to solve the problem?	YES		
12. Did the analyst test the solution presented and take action?	YES		
Close:			
13. Did the analyst give the service request record number to the customer?	YES		
14. Did the analyst use the standard close?	YES		
Customer service:			
15. Did the analyst instill confidence by using the hero statement?	YES		
16. Did the analyst transfer the call according to guidelines?	YES		
17. Did the analyst use the client's name at least once?	YES		
18. Did the analyst headline the need to put the client on hold and control hold time?	YES		
19. If the caller was angry or emotional, did the analyst handle it appropriately?	YES		
20. Did the analyst use "we" words instead of "you"?	YES		

Call and Ticket Evaluation Form – continued

	YES		NA
21. Did the analyst headline what she/he is doing during silences?			NA
22. Did the analyst speak with a friendly and polite tone?	YES		
23. Did the analyst effectively control the call?	YES		
Electronic service requests and after-call documentation			
Ticket review			
24. Did the analyst enter the customer information correctly?	YES		
25. Did the analyst properly verify the entitlement of the customer?	YES		
26. Did the analyst categorize and prioritize the service request correctly?	YES		
27. Did the analyst document the problem description accurately?	YES		
28. Was the documentation free of spelling errors and easy to understand?		NO	
29. Did the analyst document all resources checked (a knowledge base) and document troubleshooting steps taken?		NO	
30. If the call was escalated, did the analyst collect all the relevant date for effective escalation?			NA
31. Did the analyst link to the knowledge base correctly?	YES		
32. Did the analyst correctly close the record?	YES		
Totals:	24	5	3
Score:	75%		

represents the percentage of applicable elements that passed (received a yes score).

Step 4: Train and Pilot

Training should consist of two programs: one session to train the supervisors and managers who will be orchestrating this program and the service monitoring process, and another session that teach-

A dual training program is needed at this step: one for the analysts and one for the coaches.

es customer service skills included in the evaluation form. Both of these trainings are equally important.

The first training is for the supervisors and managers who will be coaching the analysts. Unless these key people receive training and education in how to position a quality program in the most positive light, you run the risk of the program failing. Analysts who are unaccustomed to service monitoring might perceive it as a "Big Brother" initiative. The supervisors and managers must have the skills to make coaching sessions a positive, educational experience for the majority of analysts who are doing a great job, and a constructive experience for those few who need to improve their skills.

The second training is for the analysts. Their training should include customer service skills training, if they have not already received it, and training on the new procedures. An ideal trainer for the new program is an analyst from the task force who understands the quality processes and the analyst's role and has the presentation skills (or potential) to facilitate the class. It is important to start the training by emphasizing the benefits of service monitoring to the analysts and how it will help them advance their careers. Appeal to their sense of purpose by tying the program to the need to serve customers better and to improve quality. Introduce the evaluation form and walk through the legend with them.

After training is completed, plan to conduct a pilot program in which you roll out the new quality program to a small group of analysts. The pilot gives you the opportunity to test new processes, gather feedback from the analysts and make changes before introducing the program to all agents. Even if you have a small group, this step should not be skipped. The feedback you gather during the pilot will help you identify glitches as well as ways to make the process better.

After a few weeks of the pilot program, the task force comes together to assess what went well and what did not, and to make any needed changes to the process before implementation. The trainer needs to incorporate any changes into the class materials, and documentation, reports and evaluation forms may need updates.

Step 5: Implement

The trainer now repeats the training program for all the analysts during the implementation phase. Careful thought must be given to the rollout to ensure that the program is received well. As discussed previously, the benefits of this program must be emphasized to the analysts in the support center. All members of the task force must be positive and convincing in both their formal and casual conversations about the program. A good way to roll out the program is with prizes for certain achievements, a party for the group or some other celebration. If funds are tight, a printed certificate of achievement and a potluck lunch are low-cost ways to recognize and celebrate together.

The Process Never Ends

A service monitoring process should be reviewed and improved periodically via feedback loops within the support center. Asking the question, "Are we really satisfying the customers and providing them with the service they want?" is a good approach to re-evaluating your program. In answering that question, some support centers find that, over time, they tend to focus too much on the technical aspects of the call, while not paying enough attention to basic customer service skills. If that is the case, a renewed emphasis on the basics of customer service is warranted. One way to tweak the call evaluation is to weight each element on the form. This is accomplished by assigning a multiplier to each question and summing the weighted scores. To re-focus the support center on customer service skills, weight the customer service questions more heavily than the procedural items.

Quality is an elusive goal, but with a solid service monitoring program in place, your support center can put a smile on your customers' faces.

Disaster Recovery

A support center is integral to a company's ability to become and stay competitive. Every support center should have a disaster recovery plan that covers, at a minimum, short- and long-term outages of all the major support tools, equipment and systems. The plan should be coordinated with the facilities department's disaster recovery plan in order to ensure that the support center is efficiently returned to service following a disaster.

The disasters that a support center must consider include:

- **Inclement weather (snow, ice, tornado, flood) that might make it difficult or impossible to commute to work.**

A support center should have a communication plan for giving instructions to analysts when there is a disaster. The plan could be for the manager to call each analyst, which means that managers need to have access to the home and cellphone numbers of each team member at all times. Another method is to tell analysts to call a special phone number that will provide instructions. You can print the phone number on an adhesive label and affix it to the back of each person's badge so they have it with them at all times.

Today, many support centers have work-at-home contingency plans in which the analysts can log in to the corporate network to access the support tools and either receive phone calls at home or retrieve customer messages from the office's voicemail system. All of these scenarios involve detailed advance planning in order to work.

- **A telephone or major system (like the service management system) outage.**

In case the service management system goes down, all analysts should have at their desk a paper version of the fields needed to enter a support request into the service management system.

If the telephone system goes down, the support center should post an announcement on the line at the telephone provider's central office that tells customers about the outage and encourages them to use electronic support.

- **Long-term outages.**

The support center needs to consider what it would do if the office is rendered inoperable for an extended amount of time. This would mean finding another location for the support center and making plans to provide access to back-up systems.

Lastly, an effective disaster recovery plan should be tested at least once a year. In some support centers, the manager secretly plans a day to announce a mock disaster and has the employees walk through the process while an observer makes note of the process and outcomes.

Best Practices – Quality Assurance

1. The support center conducts an event survey program that includes:
   a. An overall satisfaction question.
   b. A clear rating scheme using a 5-, 7- or 10-point scale.
   c. A survey that takes up to five minutes to complete.
   d. A method to exclude responders from receiving another survey for one to two months.
   e. A process to follow up on low-rated surveys.
   f. A method to include survey scores on the analyst's monthly scorecard.
2. The support center participates in a periodic survey that includes:
   a. A portion devoted to support services.
   b. An overall satisfaction question.
   c. An incentive to participate in the survey.
3. The support center sends a survey to the users of its support web site that assesses the web site's effectiveness.
4. The support center creates and regularly performs service monitoring, at least in the form of ticket monitoring.
5. The support center creates a support request evaluation and ticket evaluation form.
6. The support center has a disaster recovery plan that covers both short- and long-term outages in the center.

Organizational Management

HIRING AND SOURCING for the support center is of primary importance for an effective smaller support center. Making a poor hire in a smaller support center has vastly greater consequences than in a larger one where one person's contribution is diluted and not as visible. Superior hiring practices are the first step in retaining good people, a challenge for all support centers regardless of size. Let us explore the hiring process, outsourcing and career paths in this chapter.

Hiring

If you have been a manager for more than a month, you are probably intimately familiar with the agony of hiring. Unfortunately, most support managers get skilled in hiring good people because the support center is often an entry-level position in the company. As much as a support manager is delighted when an analyst accepts a promotion to a position outside of the support center, there is a tendency to curse the situation because of the need to hire and train a replacement for this great employee. Well, take heart in the fact that all support managers are in the same boat. The smart and experienced ones have some tips for the hiring process.

The hiring process might look like this:

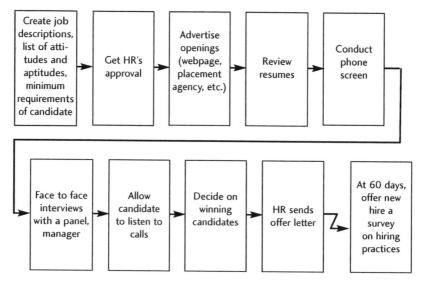

The first rule of hiring is to build the foundation for hiring. If you have not already, you must create a job description that is as thorough as possible and includes the requisite and preferred background, experience and technical skills that the job demands. In Chapter Thirteen: Training, we discuss creating a skills matrix for all your analysts. That list of skills should be included, at least in summary form, in the job description. Be sure to include on your list soft skills such as ability to learn quickly and be a team player. This list of soft skills will become the start of the "attitudes and aptitudes" that you will be looking for in new hire candidates.

Most support managers agree that hiring on attitude and aptitude is the best way to find the most successful candidates. This approach acknowledges that it is difficult to teach someone to be an empathetic, caring person who possesses the innate desire to serve customers (attitude) and that it is much easier to train someone with the ability to learn (aptitude) techni-cal subjects.

If you do not yet have a skills matrix, it is a good idea to spend time interview-ing your most successful support ana-lysts. Ask them what they think makes

Hiring on attitude and aptitude is the best way to find the most successful candidates.

them so successful on the job. Observe them in action and identify the behaviors and attitudes that contribute to their performance. For example, you might find that one characteristic of your most successful analysts is that they always show up on time and follow up with customers on or before the promised deadline. You might describe them as "trustworthy" and "punctual." If they were good at problem-solving, you would list "analytical" – and not only note that they are analytical but document how they solve problems. This will help you detect the same skills in a potential new hire.

After completing this exercise, you will have a good list of atti-tudes or qualities that you need to find in a new employee. Your list of the qualities of a good support analyst might look like this:

• Analytical	• Sense of humor	• Personable
• Empathetic	• Courageous	• Good problem-solver
• Quick learner	• Good listener	• Patient

You will also want to include aptitudes in this list, such as quick learner, because you are looking for a candidate with proficiency for learning technical subjects. Clearly, if your support environment is highly complex and technical, you will need a list of basic technical competencies to add to this list.

What if you serve a particular industry that is difficult to learn? I once worked at a software company that served the investment industry. We found that our most successful support analysts came from one of two backgrounds: either they had a strong understanding of the investment industry, or they had strong PC technical skills. As a result, we queried applicants to assess their proficiency in one or the other area and trained new hires in the area in which they had fewer skills. Even in that environment, we placed the greatest weight on attitude and aptitude over the knowledge they already possessed.

Some support organizations perceive that they do not have time to train their new hires (big mistake!) and create a long list of required technical competencies that successful candidates must possess. This causes two problems: They are probably paying more than they would to hire a less technically experienced candidate, and they may not be accepting candidates with the right attitudes to be successful.

Some support organizations perceive that they do not have time to train their new hires.

Either problem spells turnover. Those new hires will become bored quickly and leave, or you will want them to leave quickly.

Human resources may work with you in converting your list of attitudes and skills into a job description, using standard corporate forms. Of course, in some small organizations, HR assistance may not be available, in which case the support center manager must complete these tasks independently. HR may help you in benchmarking your job description to similar positions in other companies and to similar positions within the company. In this manner, salary ranges or bands are established for the position. Several standard job description samples are available in Appendix B.

After creating a job description and minimum job requirements, some organizations require that human resources get involved and approve the job description, if they have not participated in the process to this point. Follow all HR requirements, as this department can be either your best ally or a thorn in your side. Most support center managers spend time ensuring that the relationship with the HR representative is friendly and mutually helpful.

HR often helps with advertising the position opening by placing it on the corporate Intranet site and/or external web site. HR may have relationships with the online job-posting sites and with outside placement agencies that will help find candidates. Some support centers have access to an internal recruiter in the organization who can source candidates. Some of the best sources of referrals to good applicants are your existing analysts. Many organizations offer generous employee bonuses for referrals that result in a new hire. When analysts refer their friends and acquaintances, it is a win for everyone.

Some of the best sources of referrals to good applicants are your existing analysts.

The candidate wins by getting a new job, the company wins by hiring a great candidate at a lower price than working through a placement agency and the referring analyst wins a little cash in her pocket in the form of a referral fee. As the manager, do not forget to work your own contacts and networking. Jobs are often filled through the 6 degrees of separation that we all enjoy – someone knows someone who knows someone who is a good fit for the job. Local chapter meetings of associations such as HDI are fertile ground for networking. Some chapters may even post members' job openings and resumes on their web site. Don't forget your customer base as a good source of new hires. These employees show up on the first day with an understanding of the customers' environment and how the products are used in real life, and they can easily walk a mile in the customers' shoes, having already done so.

When I was managing a small support center, I found that the best new hires were friends of existing employees. The employees went out of their way to help the new hire learn the ropes and ensure that he/she was successful. After all, the employee's reputation was on the line. Especially in a small company, the word-of-mouth endorsement from happy employees is priceless. If a potential candidate hears his friend say, "I love my job – it's a great company – you should work here!" he is much more inclined to consider leaving his boring but comfortable job at a huge company to take a risk on a smaller one.

After sourcing and advertising for the job, stacks of resumes may appear on your desk. If you can afford it, the process of filtering resumes and performing phone interviews is a great one to outsource to either an internal recruiter or a placement firm. Many placement firms find that companies can advertise their positions and source candidates cheaply through web sites. The task of sorting through resumes and checking for minimum requirements is extraordinarily time-consuming, and many companies are willing to retain placement firms to do this hard work. Be sure to work closely with whomever is filtering the resumes to you, though. Make sure these individuals understand the minimum requirements of the job, the attitudes and aptitudes you are seeking, and any extras that would make a candidate especially attractive. Placement agencies are generally highly skilled at identifying your needs in a candidate, but expect to refine your working relationship and processes as you go. The process may not go as smoothly on the first hire as it does on the fifth.

When you get to face-to-face interviews, be sure to have at least two questionnaires that you follow in speaking with candidates. One should be a managerial questionnaire that contains behaviorally based interview questions designed to help the manager assess the past performance of the candidate. Unlike the mutual fund companies that say, "Past performance is no indication of future returns," hiring managers have only the past performance of a candidate upon which to base their hiring decisions. The second questionnaire might contain technical or troubleshooting questions that senior analysts pose to the candidate. Again, remember that you may be passing over good candidates if

Have at least two questionnaires that you follow in speaking with candidates.

you make the technical assessment too hard. What seems to work well in many support centers is a verbal assessment of the candidate's logical thinking and problem-solving abilities.

Some support centers conduct panel interviews for new hires with existing analysts. The advantages of this practice are that the candidate gets to meet potential future team members and the team members get a say in who will be their future teammates. If analysts interview candidates, supply them with questionnaires to fill out after the interview and be sure to include their feedback in the hiring decision-making process. A questionnaire creates a good record of the hiring effectiveness of the organization. If a new hire leaves the job prematurely or is fired, returning to the records of the interview questionnaire may provide some clues as to why this person did not succeed. The information can help the hiring team do a better job with the next hire.

If a candidate looks promising, some support centers allow the individual to sit next to an analyst and observe the employee taking phone calls. Many support centers find this decreases the person's chances of accepting a job that she does not want or will not enjoy. This practice was more common several years ago when the nature of a support center job was still relatively unknown to most candidates. As the industry has matured, more candidates arrive with previous experience supporting clients, making this practice less common.

The end of the hiring process is identifying the hirable candidates and offering them a job. Always resist the urge to hire a warm body. If your gut is telling you "No, thanks," but your head is telling

Always resist the urge to hire a warm body.

you "Hire that person — we're desperate," go with your gut. Do not try to force a candidate to fit the job. My own worst hires, and the worst hires of many of my clients and colleagues, have been desperation hires. Desperation hires usually turn into unhappy employees who are a poor match for the job.

A good way to follow up on the process is to offer new hires a hiring satisfaction survey at the end of 60 or 90 days on the job. This survey should assess the new hire's satisfaction with all aspects of the interview and new hire process, from the application form (if applicable) through the new hire training process. It is important in a competitive job market to make sure that your support center is making a good first impression with potential new employees, and the post-hire survey can help an organization find ways to improve the hiring process.

Outsourcing

When I teach support center managers, we often go through a SWOT analysis (see Chapter One: Strategic Leadership for more on SWOT analyses), which identifies strengths, weaknesses, opportunities and threats. It is interesting how many times support managers identify outsourcing as a threat to the support center. This attitude is understandable given how many jobs have been lost to outsourcing recently and the media hype about the negative aspects of offshore outsourcing. However, outsourcing can be a lifesaver for a smaller support center that cannot afford to provide after-hours support or that wishes to focus internal headcount on supporting proprietary, mission-critical applications. The concept here is finding a balance between providing support internally and strategically outsourcing some functions of the support delivery spectrum. Here are some ways to think about outsourcing a portion of your support load:

- Some internal support centers outsource support for shrink-wrapped software such as Microsoft Office. These companies generally use an ACD phone system to direct callers to the out-sourcer's support analysts. When the customers call, they hear a greeting that asks the customer to "Press 2 for support on Microsoft Office products such as Word, Excel and PowerPoint." The support center retains the support delivery for all other products. This arrangement can free up internal support personnel to concentrate on more value-added support, proprietary software support and mission-critical application support. The outsourcer chosen should have existing analysts who have deep understanding of the products they support and should be able to offer economies of scale in their pricing because they offer the same services to many companies. Many local IT firms offer this type of outsourcing.
- Some support centers, both internal and external, contract with an outsourcer to provide after-hours support. After-hours support can be expensive to provide due to the typically low utilization of the analysts who staff deep-night shifts. These employees may receive only a handful of support requests each night, but they can be important requests. Unless the analysts have other duties to perform at night, it can be a boring, lonely job that is difficult and expensive to staff. I have actually seen night-shift analysts who had taken catnaps between calls pack up their pillows and sleeping bags as they left in the morning. In a smaller environment, it is worthwhile to

consider outsourcing the deep nights. Of course, forwarding the support telephone line to a beeper or cellphone that is carried by a support analyst on a rotating basis is another common solution to after-hours support.

- Outsourcing maintenance of IT equipment such as printers and copiers is a common practice in most companies. It no longer makes sense for the IT department to maintain these machines, so companies generally contract with an outside firm to provide that service. The same can be said for some computer hardware maintenance, as many companies contract with the manufacturer to provide break/fix service on the computers.

Every company has to consider how best to use strategic outsourcing in its mix of services. However, a simple cost/benefit analysis can show which services should or should not be outsourced. A combination of complexity of the transaction and the value of the customer can create a matrix to guide your thoughts about outsourcing. The following diagram illustrates the intersection of customer value and transaction complexity in sourcing the support center.

From this diagram, we can see that smaller support centers that

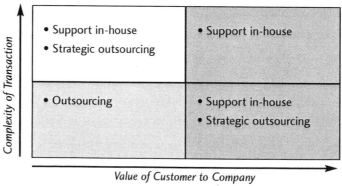

Value of Customer to Company

Sourcing Decisions for Support Centers:

provide complex support to highly valuable customers are not good candidates for outsourcing. Not only would the training burden be too great, but outsourcing would create an impediment to the close relationship needed between the support center and the development groups, which is vitally important for complex support.

Career Paths

Every support center manager has to deal with the threat of high turnover within the ranks of the support analysts. Turnover is costly; some estimates put the hard costs at 50 percent of the support analyst's annual salary, while other estimates suggest even higher rates. Experienced managers understand both the hard and soft costs of replacing a good support analyst. It can take many months for a new hire to become fully proficient and able to completely replace the contribution of the employee who left.

Creating a career path within the support center is one way to retain talent.

Creating a career path within the support center is one way to retain talent, if only for just a little longer.

The good news is that some smaller support centers have higher retention of analysts due to the job diversity inherent in a smaller organization, in which everyone needs to do a bit of everything. However, all support centers should create a career path for analysts because it recognizes the achievements of the individuals and can enhance retention.

A best practice is to create two or three position titles for the support analysts. A new support analyst begins her career in the support center as an associate (names are dependent on organizational practices), then advances to analyst I and analyst II positions. A promotion to senior analyst (also called mentor, technical advisor, etc.) recognizes the expertise of the individual and promotes that person to providing second-level support, if a tiered support model is used, or to the position of technical advisor if a touch and hold model is used.

Usually, promotion to the three levels of analyst is dependent on the speed with which the individual proceeds through training, gains demonstrable proficiency and attains the prerequisites to promotion. Promotion to senior analyst can be based on need, if the promotion mandates a transition to providing second-level support. Examples of job descriptions and the prerequisites for promotion are found in Appendix B.

It is important to recognize that not all support analysts will have the talent or desire to become a senior analyst, nor will all analysts desire to become a supervisor or take on a coordinator position. A dual career path addresses the need to provide opportunities for promotions to positions along a technical track as well as along a managerial (more people-oriented) track. Texas Instruments, a prestigious high-tech company, has formalized the dual career path. A technical engineer can advance to a position called Senior Member of the Technical Staff, the equivalent of a high-ranking manager in the organization.

A career path for a mid-sized or large support center might look like the one on the facing page.

Please note that desk-side analysts can be in a separate department in larger organizations but usually follow a similar career path to support analysts.

Smaller support centers do not have an opportunity to provide as many positions as larger ones do. In fact,

Smaller support centers can create roles that analysts assume. this diagram looks ridiculous to the manager of a support center that has fewer than 10 people in total. However, even though smaller support centers cannot create that

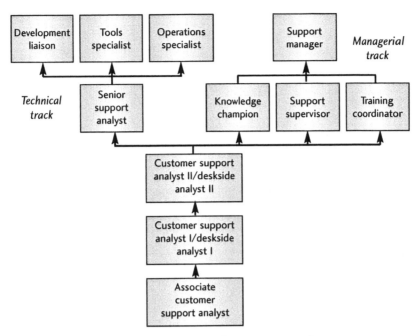

Career Path – Mid-sized and Large Support Centers

many formal positions, they can create roles that analysts assume in addition to their formal position title.

What is the difference between a role and a position? A position has a job description that describes the duties and is included in a formal career path. A role is something an employee performs as an adjunct to the formal position. From a management viewpoint, a role is more flexible than a position: You can ask people to assume roles without a promotion, you do not have to increase the employee's pay and you can expand and contract roles as needed. For the smaller support center, roles are a blessing because the manager can assign responsibility for the many tasks that need to be done in the support center. Roles also help fill in the downtime between calls that is more prevalent in a smaller support center.

To illustrate how a smaller support center can use roles, an analyst II might be designated as the knowledge champion or the training coordinator (see Chapter Thirteen: Training and Chapter Six: Knowledge Management for the responsibilities of these roles) or a senior analyst might also be the tools specialist. Other analysts might be asked to provide support to the training coordinator or tools specialist from time to time or as an ongoing responsibility. For

A great joy of working in smaller support center is the job diversity provided by assigning roles to each analyst.

the small internal support center, a best practice is to rotate the job of providing desktop support, which characterizes desk-side support as a role instead of a position. See Chapter Fourteen: Staffing and Scheduling for more information on creating a formal rotation schedule. This is a joy of working in a smaller support center – to provide job diversity for every analyst using roles.

The smaller support center needs to accomplish the same work that a larger one does and can do so by assigning roles to analysts.

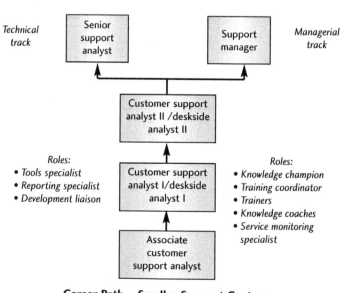

Career Path – Smaller Support Centers

Best Practices — Organizational Management

1. Hire for attitudes and aptitudes, not technical knowledge. You can teach employees the technical skills, but it is much harder to teach soft skills.
2. Create job descriptions for each position in the support center.
3. One of the best sources for new hires is employee referrals.
4. At 60 days' post-hire date, offer new employees a survey to assess the effectiveness of your hiring process.
5. Consider strategic outsourcing of non-critical products or after-hours support.
6. Create a career path for all support analysts.
7. Use roles instead of positions in the smaller center to provide job diversity.
8. Rotate roles periodically.

## CHAPTER TWELVE

Team Management

IN A SMALLER SUPPORT CENTER, the concept of teamwork is important to the success of the group. With a smaller group, there is greater opportunity to forge strong bonds among analysts, to have fun together and to provide outstanding support. In this chapter, we explore some of the ways a manager can promote teamwork and create a supportive work environment.

Team Communications and Meetings

A best practice in the support community is to provide regular times for team meetings, at least once monthly. The team meeting should be a time for the manager to reinforce communications that were sent via email, to review progress toward goals and to build teamwork.

Here are some ideas for team meeting agendas:

- A brainteaser or quick team-building exercise to break the ice. A good resource for team-building exercises is a book by Brian Cole Miller called *Quick Team-Building Activities for Busy Managers*.[13]

---

[13] *Brian Cole Miller,* Quick Team-Building Activities for Busy Managers *(New York: AMACOM, 2004)*

- Review of departmental communications and news.
- Recognition of outstanding team members with "spot" awards or a review of those analysts who received spot awards since the last meeting.
- Talk about challenging situations encountered by each of the team members.
- A book or article report presented by team members.
- A quick training module on commonly asked questions, presented by a team member or the team lead.

Rewards and Recognition

As you ponder how to build a highly functional team, remember this discovery from the scientific approach to human actions called "behaviorism." This school of thought has established that behavior that is recognized and rewarded will be repeated. Also true, as pointed out by Ferdinand F. Fournies in his book *Coaching for Improved Work Performance*[14] is the other side of the coin: Behavior that is ignored will decrease in frequency. This advice squares with our awareness of our own behaviors. When we feel like no one notices the good job we do, at home or at work, we feel resentful and highly unlikely to keep up the effort. When my husband cleans the kitchen floor or cuts the grass, I am quick to express my gratitude because I want him to do it again in the future. If I clean the house and he does not notice, I have a tendency to fish for recognition with, "Did you notice anything different about the house, dear?" The wise manager will be constantly on the lookout for ways to recognize good deeds and behavior in an effort to reproduce it. Whatever the manager identifies as worthy of recognition will be noted by co-workers.

There are several ways to work recognition into the daily routine

[14] *Ferdinand F. Fournies, Coaching for Improved Work Performance (New York: McGraw-Hill, 2000)*

of the support center. All supervisors and managers should practice MBWA (management by wandering around) as popularized by Tom Peters in the groundbreaking book, *In Search of Excellence*.[15] While wandering around, the manager should be on the lookout for positive behavior and should take time to personally acknowledge the behavior and thank the person. Accentuating the positive is one of the quickest ways in a smaller support center to change group behavior.

> **All supervisors and managers should practice MBWA.**

Some support managers print complimentary emails they receive from customers, write a note of appreciation on them and post them to a "Wall of Fame" or bulletin board in the support center. If analysts go beyond the call of duty, a nice way to recognize them is to send a hand-written note to the home address, thanking them for their performance. In this way, the entire family is likely to know that Mom or Dad is receiving praise from the manager.

You can also institutionalize the practice of "catch someone doing something right" by allowing peers to recognize each other. When I managed a small support center, we printed forms such as the ones found in Appendix D (we rotated between the forms), gave a stack of them to each person in the support center and encouraged analysts to complete a form whenever they observed a colleague exhibiting outstanding behavior. We posted the forms on a bulletin board in the break room, and I regularly recognized all recipients at our team meetings to great applause.

Whenever giving recognition to someone, be sure to use his name, look him in the eye if you are communicating in person, describe precisely what he did well and either thank him or tell him how you feel about his performance. The specific description of the positive behavior is extremely important, both for the individual

---

[15] *Tom Peters,* In Search of Excellence: Lessons From America's Best-Run Companies *(New York: HarperCollins, 2004)*

and for the team. This description tells everyone exactly what was good and what behavior to repeat. Vague compliments such as "Good job handling the call from Mr. Johnson" are not as effective as "I really liked how you used empathy to handle Mr. Johnson during that last call. I actually heard you empathize with him three times before things seem to calm down. Good job!"

Specific description of the positive behavior is extremely important.

Some support centers create rewards based on the monthly analyst scorecard. They recognize the highest scoring analysts each month and may note the most improved analysts or analysts who achieve a personal best score (as compared to their historic scores).

Coaching

The support manager or supervisor accomplishes things through others. This means that a manager must communicate, motivate, teach, direct and discipline their employees. Coaching is a process that enables these activities. The term coaching carries connotations from sports, in which a coach helps players improve their game by offering observations, advice, analysis and lessons on skills that the player needs in order to be successful. Coaching in business has the same purpose – to help employees improve their skills and be more successful in their careers.

There are two approaches to coaching: far and near. Every coach or manager should always start by using the far approach with an employee. Far implies a dialogue in which the coach is curiously seeking information, assessing the situation and deciding on the best course of action with input from the analyst. The far approach assumes no blame, is positive and can be a teaching opportunity. The near approach is taken after several far encounters and only when the manager has repeatedly observed undesirable behaviors and has done adequate research to draw reasonable conclusions. The near approach is a monologue that includes the emotions of the manager. Over a series of coaching encounters, managers may draw increasingly near in their approach, so it is not a black-and-white decision as to which to use. However, we will describe far and near coaching processes as if they are separate sequences of actions, with the understanding that the astute manager will choose steps appropriate to the situation.

There are two approaches to coaching: far and near.

Far Coaching Process

This process is invoked in a number of situations: after monitoring and evaluating an analyst's phone call or electronic support request, during scheduled one-on-one meetings, or when the manager observes some behavior that is outside of acceptable bounds, such as the analyst is repeatedly late to work.

Unlike what many new managers might envision, the coaching process is a deliberate, well-planned exercise. Shooting from the hip is not recommended, especially for newer managers. Rather, a good deal of thought and preparation will ensure that the process goes smoothly.

On a high level, the coaching process looks like this:

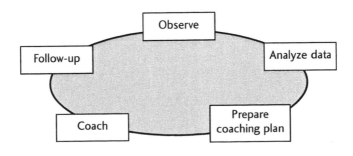

Observe

This five-step process starts with an observation of the analyst in action. Observations can come from a variety of situations:

- Listening to a recorded interaction with a customer while performing service monitoring.
- Observing the analyst during a team meeting, for example, while she is making a presentation to the team or participating in a discussion.
- Observing the analyst performing the job.
- Reviewing reports of job performance.
- Indirect observation, through reports or complaints from team members, other managers or customers.

Indirect observations require caution on the part of the manager, because it is difficult to discuss behavior that was only reported to the manager. In these cases, the manager must collect numerous data points before drawing conclusions.

Analyze Data

For service monitoring, this step involves scoring an evaluation form that lists the expectations of the analyst during a customer interaction. (An example of a call evaluation form is found later in this chapter.) Managers may wish to listen to the call recording or read the support request record multiple times to make sure they understand all the nuances of the particular interaction.

For other observed behaviors, the manager may wish to seek previous records, such as historical performance reports and annual performance reviews. A thorough review of current data from the telephone, service management system and other tools is required. The manager must have a thorough understanding of the data available.

Prepare Coaching Plan

Preparing to coach is an important step, especially if the coaching session will be focused on performance improvements. The following coaching form can be used to prepare for the conversation.

Coaching Planning Form

Analyst: _____ Coaching date: _____
Coach: _____ Call date (if applicable) _____

Strengths:

1. _____

2. _____

3. _____

Opportunities for improvement

1. _____

_____

_____

Start/stop/continue (optional):

Start: _____

_____

Stop: _____

_____

Continue: _____

_____

Probing questions:

1. _____

2. _____

3. _____

Possible training needed:

1. _____

2. _____

Description of improved behavior:

1. _____

2. _____

Follow-up date/time:

1. _____

2. _____

This coaching form helps the manager organize thoughts about the coaching session. Alternatively, you may wish to incorporate the coaching form into the call evaluation form, such as in this example:

Call and Ticket Evaluation Form

Analyst:
Supervisor:
Meter number: (where to find the call recording, if applicable)
Date:

Call segment:	YES	NO	N/A
Greeting:			
1. Was standard greeting used?	YES		
Problem identification:			
2. Did the analyst actively listen to customer?		NO	
3. Did the analyst paraphrase and confirm the problem description?	YES		
4. Did the analyst ask appropriate questions to properly identify the problem?		NO	
Analysis:			
5. Did the analyst ask appropriate questions to explore conditions and troubleshoot?	YES		
6. Did the analyst effectively use his/her resources to research possible solutions?	YES		
7. Did the analyst replicate the customer's problem?	YES		
8. Did the analyst follow escalation guidelines and escalate when appropriate?			NA
Resolution:			
9. Did the analyst educate the customer on how to use the self-service knowledge base?		NO	
10. Did the analyst state the resolution plan in a clear manner?	YES		
11. Did the analyst walk the customer through the steps to solve the problem?	YES		
12. Did the analyst test the solution presented and take action?	YES		
Close:			
13. Did the analyst give the service request record number to the customer?	YES		
14. Did the analyst use the standard close?	YES		
Customer service:			
15. Did the analyst instill confidence by using the hero statement?	YES		
16. Did the analyst transfer the call according to guidelines?	YES		
17. Did the analyst use the client's name at least once?	YES		
18. Did the analyst headline the need to put the client on hold and control hold time?	YES		
19. If the caller was angry or emotional, did the analyst handle it appropriately?	YES		
20. Did the analyst use "we" words instead of "you"?	YES		

Call and Ticket Evaluation Form – continued

21. Did the analyst headline what she/he is doing during silences?			NO
22. Did the analyst speak with a friendly and polite tone?	YES		
23. Did the analyst effectively control the call?	YES		
Electronic Service Requests and After-Call Documentation			
Ticket Review			
24. Did the analyst enter the customer information correctly?	YES		
25. Did the analyst properly verify the entitlement of the customer?	YES		
26. Did the analyst categorize and prioritize the service request correctly?	YES		
27. Did the analyst document the problem description accurately?	YES		
28. Was the documentation free of spelling errors and easy to understand?		NO	
29. Did the analyst document all resources checked (a knowledge base) and document troubleshooting steps taken?		NO	
30. If the call was escalated, did the analyst collect all the relevant date for effective escalation?			NA
31. Did the analyst link to the knowledge base correctly?	YES		
32. Did the analyst correctly close the record?	YES		
Totals:	24	4	3
Score:	75%		
Strengths or start/stop/continue			
1			
2			
3			
Opportunity for improvement			
Proving, non-threatening questions			
1			
2			
3			
Followup date/time and notes			

In a far conversation, it is necessary to point out at least one positive aspect of the observed behavior. In service monitoring it is often easy to identify two or three strengths of the analyst in serving the customer. On page 199, only two spaces are provided for opportunities for improvement because the analyst can only concentrate on one or two aspects of performance at a time. Throwing the book at an individual is counter-productive, as it only overwhelms and demoralizes the person. An alternative to identifying strengths and opportunities for improvement is to conduct a "start/stop/continue" exercise in which the manager identifies behaviors to start, to stop and to continue. This is a helpful structure for some managers, as it encapsulates the coaching process into one easy-to-remember phrase.

In the right column of the coaching planning form is a section that helps the manager identify probing questions to ask during the discussion. The purpose of questioning is to direct the analyst in analyzing his performance and to have the individual define improvements and next steps. It is a fact that people who come to their own conclusions are better convinced than if someone else tells them what to think or do. Some examples of probing questions are:

- How might you do that differently in the future?
- What do you think the customer really wanted or needed?
- How do you feel about this?
- Do you think you are adequately trained on that topic?
- What outcome were you looking for?
- What needs to be done?
- How can I help?
- What are some reasons that may not have worked as well as you hoped?

In planning the coaching session, the manager may suspect that the individual needs training and should use the training section of the planning form for that. The last two sections ask for a specific description of the improved behavior including metrics (if applicable) and a date for a follow-up session with the analyst. If improvements are needed, the follow-up meeting should be scheduled in two weeks.

Coach

Now that the coaching planning form is complete, the manager conducts the actual coaching session. The manager should explain the reason for the coaching, as in "Let's set a time for our monthly one-on-one session to review service monitoring results."

Support managers should consider the following:

- During the first few coaching sessions, the manager should demonstrate that coaching is a career development aid. The manager should make the experience overwhelmingly positive in order to overcome any fears about coaching. Making small-talk to get the conversation started (as in, "So, how's the family?" or "How's your baseball team doing?") can put the analyst at ease, build rapport and allow the manager to learn about the analyst's personal life. The manager should ensure that the analyst understands the benefits of coaching and the opportunity it provides for career development.

- Offer observations of the negative behavior in question. Use your five senses to describe it, but do not include emotions in the expression. You might say, "I hear an edge in your voice when you respond to the customer" or "I saw you pound your fist on the desk" or "I see on our phone reports that you have arrived at least 15 minutes late on each of the last five Monday mornings."

- Ensure understanding of the importance of the skill or behavior. This may be best initiated with a probing question such as, "Why do you think it is important to use a standard greeting when answering the phone?" If the analyst does not understand the importance, the manager needs to explain it.

- Ensure the analyst understands the consequences of doing versus not doing the skill or behavior in terms of "what's in it for me" (WII-FM). Assess the analyst's understanding with a probing question, and make sure the individual knows the benefits of the expected behavior. For example, "What do you think are the advantages to everyone using a standard greeting in the support center?"

- Ensure the analyst knows how to perform the skill. If the analyst indicates that she does not know how to perform the task, provide training on the spot or arrange for training as soon as possible. For example, you may say, "Hmm, so you are not familiar with empathy statements. Let's go over a few right now so you can write them down and then choose one or two that you'd like to practice during the next week."
- Assess the analyst's motivation to perform the skills.
- Then, teach, direct or make a suggestion or an observation. Make an assignment and set a time to follow up (no more than two weeks out).

Near Coaching Process

A manager uses a near approach when it is observed that a negative behavior continues despite previous coaching sessions. The ultimate near conversation is the termination meeting, in which the manager must fire the employee. However, in this process we assume that the employee has not done anything that would necessitate an immediate termination, with the understanding that the near coaching process may ultimately end in a termination meeting.

Before starting a near coaching session, the manager must be sure of his facts.

Before starting a near coaching session, the manager must be sure of his facts. This conversation should be the culmination of several successively nearer coaching conversations, in which it is clear that the analyst is not performing to expectations.

The near process starts with calling the analyst into a private office for the conversation. It is important that a near coaching session is not conducted in a place where others can see or hear the encounter; conducting this session privately protects the analyst from embarrassment and from others hearing personal information. The manager should arrange the meeting for as soon as possible after observing the behavior, or as soon as the manager is able to control her emotions about the incident. The manager must be able to express emotions but not be controlled by them. This may mean sleeping on it before confronting the analyst.

Start by describing the unsatisfactory behavior. Use your observation skills, as described above. Name a specific instance that illustrates the negative behavior. You might say, "I need to talk to you about what I observed last night before the end of the shift. I heard you raise your voice to a customer, slam your fist on the desk and hang up." Explain that this behavior does not meet your expectations, which you have explained before.

Next, describe how the analyst's behavior makes you feel. The best way to express this is with an "I" statement, in which you describe how you feel in relation to the observed behavior. You might say, "I am frustrated that this behavior continues. I am also angry and embarrassed that I continue to receive negative feedback about you from our customers." Expressing your emotions is honest and makes the analyst aware of the consequences of the negative behavior. It also conveys the gravity of the situation.

Expressing your emotions conveys the gravity of the situation.

Then you should state why this issue is so important. Point out what is at stake for the support center, for the analyst and for the manager. You might say, "Our reputation with our customers in the past has not been good, and we need everyone in the support center to present a positive image in order to turn that around."

End your monologue with a wish to resolve the issue and then ask the analyst to respond. You might say, "I want to resolve this issue as soon as possible – the issue with your lack of patience and empathy with our customers. Please tell me what you plan to do about it."

In a near coaching session, Susan Scott, in her book *Fierce Conversations*, points out that the traditional "sandwich" approach does not work.[16] The sandwich approach suggests that you start and end with a positive observation about the analyst, and sandwich the negative into the middle. She contends that this dilutes the message and confuses the analyst. It is best to save the niceties for when they are warranted and keep the conversation as stern as the situation demands.

The Follow-up

The last step in the coaching process is the follow-up. In your session, you and the analyst have agreed on action steps to take to improve the analyst's performance. The worst thing you can do at this time is to forget about it and assume that the change happens. Right in the coaching session, schedule a follow-up date and time that is no more than two weeks away. Note on the coaching planning form both the date of the next session and exactly what you will be taking about. This follow-up prevents the manager from being the "seagull" manager that Ken Blanchard describes. The seagull manager swoops in, makes a big mess, then flies off, never to be seen again.[17]

---

[16] *Susan Scott,* Fierce Conversations: Achieving Success at Work & in Life One Conversation at a Time *(New York: The Berkley Publishing Group, 2002)*

[17] *Ken Blanchard and Don Shula,* The Little Book of Coaching: Motivating People To Be Winners *(New York: HarperCollins, 2001)*

Best Practices – Team Management

1. The support center should conduct team meetings at least once a month.

2. Rewards and recognition for positive behavior are integral to ensuring that those behaviors continue. The support center will have a program that includes both formal and informal recognition of outstanding performance.

3. Making the support center a fun environment helps create a supportive work environment and can improve customer service.

4. The manager coaches each analyst at least once monthly.

5. Far and near coaching techniques are used appropriately.

## CHAPTER THIRTEEN

Training

NO MATTER THE SIZE of the support center, a good training program, consisting of both a new hire training program and ongoing training for more experienced analysts, is imperative. Many studies have shown that IT and technology workers value training that keeps their skills up-to-date over many other employee benefits. Fortunately, there are ways to embed training into the regular tasks of the support center so that every support center is able to provide at least informal training. The support center that builds a strong training program benefits in the following ways:

- **The creation of a culture of continuous learning and knowledge-sharing.** It is important that each person in the support center understands that his job is to serve customers, solve problems and share knowledge with co-workers.
- **Improved teamwork.** Through knowledge-sharing and collaborative problem-solving, the team is strengthened.
- **Increased efficiency of the support center.** Better-trained analysts can solve more problems, which increases first contact

resolution or first-level resolution rates and reduces the time to resolution for the customer.

- **Better retention of analysts.** If analysts understand that management will invest in their skills, they feel appreciated and tend to stay in the job. Employees do not come to work to fail – and analysts fail to solve customer issues if they are not adequately and continuously trained.

Support centers need someone who will coordinate training, a way to determine what training is needed, a plan for new hire and continuous training, and a continuously evolving library of training materials.

Training Coordinator

Every support center needs a training coordinator, whether it is a full-time position or a role that the manager or a support analyst plays. Large support centers may have a complete staff of trainers dedicated to providing new hire and ongoing training for the support center staff. The large center may use advanced tools such as a learning management system that tracks and coordinates the training classes planned and completed by analysts. Generally, these larger organizations have access to online and facilitator-led training modules offered through a third-party vendor. Some smaller support centers may have access to these tools and outside training opportunities through the auspices of the larger corporation. However, many smaller support centers cannot afford the luxury of a dedicated, full-time training coordinator. The duties of a training coordinator can be assigned to an analyst as an additional, part-time role that that person plays in addition to supporting customers. The

Many smaller support centers cannot afford the luxury of a dedicated, full-time training coordinator.

manager may perform the role of the training coordinator by default, but this is a good role to delegate to an experienced analyst who has a natural ability to teach and explain concepts to others.

The training coordinator should be responsible for:

- **Assessing training needs.** There are several ways to do this, including using skills gap analysis, employing service monitoring data, consulting the calendar of scheduled product releases to plan for new-product training, and others.

- **Coordinating training facilitators.** This includes identifying someone to create the training materials and facilitate the training.

- **Scheduling training.** This means working with the manager to determine the best time for training, given the support center's workload and analysts' schedules. The training coordinator should keep a calendar of training sessions, both for future planning and for reporting. This can be done simply in a spreadsheet that records the name of the session, the date and the attendees.

- **Ensuring the quality of the training.** A best practice is to provide evaluations at the end of each training session. The evaluation would assess the course materials, the abilities of the facilitator and the content of the class.

- **Assessing the learning of the students.** In larger support centers, post-learning quizzes or certifications are created to test the knowledge of the participants. In smaller centers, this can be done through informal observation or through service monitoring and coaching.

- **Recording the attendees at each training session.** The training coordinator must ensure that all analysts who need the training attend it. The record should be used to report the training activity. (Note that training hours is a metric on the support center balanced scorecard in Chapter Nine: Metrics and Reporting.) Many support centers record training sessions with either a video camera or audio recording equipment so that analysts on the night shift, for example, are able to view the training at a later time. At a minimum, the training materials should be given to those who are not present for the class.

- **Reporting the success of the training program.** This may be as simple as reporting to the manager on how many training sessions were completed during a quarter or year. If management declares that learning is important to the support center, reporting the training completed is the way to prove it.

Skills Matrix Analysis

In a small support center, the manager probably knows the skills and strengths of each support analyst just by working closely together and hearing the analysts take phone calls. Training needs are easy to assess in that case. For example, the manager may notice that the analyst has trouble understanding the customer's environment because that person has not worked in the industry before. The manager may ask the training coordinator to arrange for the analyst to visit a customer's office for a morning and observe how the customer uses technology.

In a support center in which the manager or training coordinator does not hear every call, a more formal method to identify training needs is necessary. The first way is through service monitoring, in which the coach may identify opportunities for individual training, either refresher or original training. For example, in a service monitoring session, the coach may observe that the analyst does not understand how to reset a printer queue, so training on that topic can be arranged for the individual. If many analysts are having trouble with the same issue, the training coordinator should schedule a refresher class.

Another way to assess training needs is to conduct a skills analysis, in which each analyst's skills levels are measured. This is typically done at the beginning of the year, and the results feed into both the individual's training plan and the group training plan. To create a skills assessment, the manager and training coordinator create a list of skills that a good analyst should possess. In a small support center, the training coordinator may already know what the needed skills are. If not, a good way to create a list of necessary skills is to interview a handful of the best analysts in the support center and ask them what skills they use in providing support. Then, observe these star performers doing their jobs. Listen to their phone calls to discern some of the customer service or soft skills they employ to handle customers.

Another way to assess training needs is to conduct a skills analysis.

After this discovery period, the training coordinator can create a list of skills needed for success as a support center analyst. The skills can be organized in categories such as customer service skills, hardware skills and software skills. The skills might look like this:

List of Skills

Customer service skills	Hardware skills	Software skills, Microsoft Office	Software skills, accounting
• Listening	• Dell laptops	• Outlook	• Payroll
• Empathy	• Dell desktops	• Exchange	• AP
• Paraphrasing	• LAN	• Word	• GL
• Questioning	• Wan	• Excel	• Fixed assets
• Troubleshooting	• Telephony	• PowerPoint	• AR
• Using standard greeting	• Connectivity	• Access	
• Closing call effectively			

Once you have a list of skills, convert the list to a spreadsheet and provide it to the analysts to self-score. Some support centers use a 5-point scale for the assessment where 1 is a novice and 5 is an expert. Be sure to define the criteria for each rating. The manager or technical lead should also assess the skills of each analyst. Results can be recorded in a spreadsheet, with tabs for each category.

Skills Matrix – Customer Service Skills

Skill:	Listening		Empathy		Paraphrasing		Questioning		Trouble-shooting		Using standard greeting		Closing call		Average
	Mgr	Self	Mgr	Self	Mgr	Self	Mgr	Self	Mgr	Self	Mgr	Self	Mgr	Self	
Analyst 1	4	5	3	4	4	4	5	4	4	4	4	3	2	1	4.00
Analyst 2	2	3	3	3	4	4	5	5	5	5	5	5	5	5	4.08
Analyst 3	5	5	4	5	3	3	4	4	2	3	5	5	5	5	4.00
Analyst 4	3	5	1	2	4	4	4	5	4	4	4	4	4	4	3.67
Analyst 5	5	4	5	4	5	5	5	5	5	5	4	5	4	5	4.75
Analyst 6	4	5	4	5	4	5	4	4	4	4	5	5	5	5	4.42
Analyst 7	3	3	3	4	4	3	4	3	4	4	5	5	5	5	3.75
Analyst 8	5	5	4	4	5	5	3	3	3	4	3	5	4	4	4.08
Analyst 9	4	4	4	4	5	3	3	3	3	3	5	5	5	5	3.83
Analyst 10	5	4	5	5	5	5	5	5	4	4	4	4	4	4	4.58
Averages:	4	4.3	3.6	4	4.3	4.1	4.2	4.1	3.8	4	4.4	4.6	4.3	4.3	4.12

By averaging the columns (which represent the team's skills levels) and the rows (which represent individual analyst's skills), the training coordinator and manager can identify the skills that the team needs to develop and can identify individual training opportunities for the analysts. In the example above, empathy is the lowest rated customer service skill for the team, which would tell the training coordinator that a refresher class on empathy skills is needed. The training coordinator can use this to create training plans for the support center for the coming year. The manager can use this information to develop individual training plans for each support analyst.

New Hire Training

OK, so now that you have some new hires, what are you going to do with them – throw them on the phones right after their orientation session with human resources? It is unreasonable to expect new hires to read the manual and sit with an experienced analyst in an informal manner in order to be equipped to handle phone calls or installations. Tempting as it may be, the absence of a well-organized new hire plan is not optimal, even for the brightest new analysts. Employee development starts the moment a person is hired and never ends.

To create a new hire training program, the training coordinator can enlist the best support analysts to help build an outline of all the knowledge that a new analyst will need to know. You may wish to refer to the skills matrix created in the previous section. Include technical skills, how to use internal tools such as the service management system, processes for handling calls, and what you need to know about the business or needs of the typical customer. Do not forget soft skills, such as problem-solving methods, how to handle an angry client and how to control a customer who wants to tell you all about the grandchild's piano recital.

Important Consideration:

Providing support analysts with only customer training (traiing designed to teach customers how to use the supported products)is not sufficient. Support analysts must have more in-depth training to understand how the software works (as opposed to how to use the software) and they need troubleshooting training. In addition, support analysts need technical information on topics such as operating systems and databases. Many companies mistakenly equate customer training with support analyst training.

Now, using the outline of skills, the training coordinator should develop a new hire training plan. A combination of study methods is best, including attending one-on-one or classroom training with experienced support analysts, observing someone doing the job, reading materials, doing exercises, etc. It is OK to include self-study in your plan, such as reading a manual and testing the concepts on a computer, or completing a computer-based training (CBT) module – as long as there is someone for the new hire to go to when she needs a question answered. The training coordinator or a mentor should be available to guide new hires through their initial training.

The training coordinator might produce a standard new hire training schedule that references other materials and identifies the persons responsible for teaching each module. A simple new hire training schedule might look like this:

Sample Training Schedule

Day 1	Morning	HR orientation: time sheets, benefits, paperwork. Lunch with support center manager.	HR Support manager
	Afternoon	Support center orientation: Processes, training schedule, who does what, org chart, etc.	Support manager
Days 2 – 5	Morning	Study manual on X topic, also training materials on same topic.	Mentor
	Afternoon	Sit with a senior, product manager or developer to discuss X topic.	Suzy
Days 6 – 10	All day	Attend customer training.	Customer training coordinator
Days 11 – 14	Morning	Study training materials.	Self-study
	Afternoon	Listen to calls with mentor, take calls with mentor listening.	Pete
Day 15	All day	Visit a local client to observe how the software is used in real life.	Michelle coordinates
Days 16 – 20	Morning	Take calls.	With mentor
	Afternoon	Review calls with senior analyst.	Alan
Days 21 – 25	Morning	Take calls.	With mentor
	Afternoon	Supervisor monitors two calls per day, discusses them with new hire at the end of each day.	Sharon

A good way to structure the new hire's transition to taking phone calls is to have him gradually take on more responsibility. This is more successful than a "sink or swim" approach to taking phone calls, in which the analyst is told to start taking calls independently before he is fully trained and confident. Some support centers assign each new hire to a mentor who is responsible for conducting the new hire's transition to the phones. Other support centers prefer that a new hire sit with several experienced analysts during the transition time, to get exposure to different approaches and areas of expertise.

Each step in this process should be measured in days. The process might look like this:

- Step 1: The new hire listens to an experienced analyst for a few hours at a time.
- Step 2: The new hire listens and documents the support request in the support system for the analyst (mentor) who is taking the call.
- Step 3: The new hire talks on the phone with the customer while the mentor documents the call.
- Step 4: The new hire talks and types while the mentor listens.
- Step 5: The new hire takes calls independently, but the supervisor reviews all calls at the end of the day.

Ongoing Training

An effective training program does not stop with new hire training. Creating an environment of continual learning has many benefits, including an increase in employee retention. Depending on corporate resources that are available, you can create a simple, low-cost, ongoing training program, or you can encourage your employees to take advantage of corporate training programs.

Many corporations offer a tremendous benefit to employees by reimbursing the costs of formal educational degrees. I have a friend whose company is paying for his MBA at a local university. This person is totally committed to that company for at least two years, when he will finish his degree – what a great retention strategy. Your company may also offer certification training, such as the Microsoft certifications. If your company offers such programs, by all means encourage your employees to take advantage of them.

Many small support centers do not have access to formal training and complain that they do not have a budget for training. Each support center, however, has smart analysts who can teach each other what they know and learn. Experts agree that until an employee teaches a skill, that person does not thoroughly understand the skill. It is in this light that the following recommendations are made.

As one person learns technical or application skills, the support center should expect that person to teach it to others. "Each one teach one" (in the sense that each person teaches one class to many students) is an effective slogan for a support center.

Each One Teach One

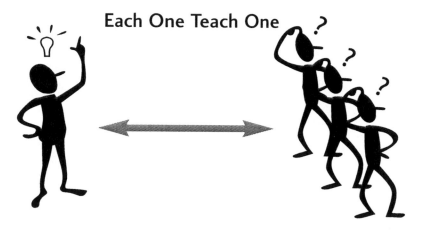

Topics for technical training will vary depending on the support center, but there is no end of in-depth training topics an analyst could present. Training topics will come naturally out of the issues that each person handles and the expertise that each analyst develops.

Soft skills such as customer service skills, communication skills, time management, etc., can also be taught in the team meetings. One effective way to accomplish this is to institute a program of book or article reviews presented during the team meeting. The manager might ask each analyst to prepare and present a book report once a quarter. The books could be on any relevant subject to the support center, but a good topic to present a report on is customer service skills or other soft skills. The analyst should prepare a short presentation, complete with exercises for the team.

No- or Low-Cost Training Ideas

In addition to training during the support center's team meeting, here are some other ideas for providing ongoing training at minimal expense:

- **Brown bag lunches:** Many companies use a simple brown bag lunch format in which experts from either inside or outside the support center present a short class on their subject. This is a great way to share knowledge and provide a developmental opportunity for senior analysts.

- **Apprenticeships:** Apprentice your analysts to a third-level analyst or IT analyst (if you are an in-house support center) or to a programmer or developer (if you are an external support center). The apprentices can shadow their "masters," observing how they troubleshoot problems and assisting with project work. In an external support center, your apprentices can test new releases of your product or support customer beta testing programs.

- **Computer-based training:** Many companies have libraries of CBTs on a variety of technical subjects. Encourage your analysts to complete these programs during their off-phone times.

- **Lab time:** Set up a computer lab in your center for analysts to visit during their off-phone times. This offers them an opportunity not only to apply what they have learned during their training sessions, but also to work on resolutions to customers problems.

- **Book reports:** As you become aware of books or publications on topics related to your business, ask various analysts to read them and report to the group or their team. You could start your own set of *CliffsNotes* for the important publications in your field.

- **Student returns as teacher:** Small support centers can never afford to send everyone to outside training, even if it is needed. A good example of training that everyone needs is on a major operating system upgrade, such as Windows Vista. The small support center can send one person to Microsoft training, then have that person return to the office and prepare a training class for the rest of the support team. Be careful not to violate copyright laws, but create materials that are customized to the organization's specific needs.

- **Free video resources:** Your public library may have videos on motivational subjects, customer service or other topics. Show the videos during team meetings and prepare exercises or discussion questions for after the viewing. Business authors are beginning to augment their publications with web-based videos. In *The Eighth Habit*,[18] Stephen Covey offers free video segments on his web site. This book and the accompanying video vignettes could make excellent discussion topics for several support team meetings.

Many years ago, one clever analyst I managed found he could get a demonstration copy of a video made by a famous motivational business speaker. He could have the video for only two days before he

---

[18] *Stephen R. Covey, The Eighth Habit: From Effectiveness to Greatness (New York: Free Press, 2004)*

would be charged for it. He carefully planned when to order the video so it arrived in time for the support center's all-day retreat. The entire team viewed the video and had a lively discussion afterward. The analyst mailed the video back to the speaker on our way home from the retreat. I do not know of a speaker who is doing that anymore, but a bright person can be on the lookout for similar opportunities to train on a dime.

As you get sophisticated with your ongoing training program, consider coordinating it with your career path within the support center. For example, the requirements for being considered for a promotion might include completing a group of CBTs and being the subject-matter expert for two brown bag lunches. These accomplishments show mastery of a subject and could be one of many criteria used in assessing an analyst's preparation for advancement within your center.

Career Planning

With each analyst in the support center, create an individual career plan once a year. This career plan should include long-range and short-term goals, a list of skills needed to accomplish those goals and the steps necessary to achieve them. Create a career-planning form that is relevant to your company's situation and have each analyst complete this form prior to the annual review. Track each individual's progress toward his or her goals during monthly one-on-one meetings. Be an advocate for each employee by looking for advancement opportunities, both within your center and within the company.

Jump-start your employee development program by offering new hire training, ongoing training and career planning to your analysts. Your efforts will be rewarded in many ways, including happier analysts and happier customers – both of which are good for business.

Best Practices — Training

1. Identify a training coordinator. For small support centers, this is most likely a role; for mid-sized centers, it could be a position.

2. Create a skills matrix for analysts and use it to identify skills needed in new hires and to determine training plans for existing analysts.

3. Create a formal new hire training program. It is not sufficient to send analysts to customer training or to offer only job-shadowing before taking support requests independently.

4. Ease new hires into their jobs by assigning them a mentor who helps them gradually take on more responsibility in serving customers.

5. Create an ongoing training program. Use low- or no-cost methods that include an "each one, teach one" philosophy that enables analysts to learn, then share their knowledge with others.

## CHAPTER FOURTEEN

Staffing and Scheduling

HOW MANY ANALYSTS are needed for a support center? When should they be scheduled to work? Every support center needs to answer these questions. Since employee salaries and benefits represent 70 percent or more of a support center's budget, the question of how many analysts are needed is one of utmost importance. Overstaffing the support center is costly for the company, and understaffing is costly for the customers (in increased wait times for service) and the support center (in terms

> **Employee salaries and benefits represent 70 percent or more of a support center's budget.**

of burnout and attrition). Once a staffing level is determined, then the support center needs to decide how best to deploy the analysts, according to the anticipated workload. In this chapter, we will explore how to estimate how many analysts are needed in the support center and how to schedule them to maximize productivity.

How Many Analysts Do We Need?

Several methods answer this question in the support center.

Some support centers are given a fixed budget within which to work that determines how many employees can be hired. That is called cost-based hiring and is not recommended, however common it may be. Another method is the ratio-based model, in which the number of customers served is equated to the number of needed analysts. You may have seen something like this ratio model:

Ratio Model – Example

Technology environment supported	Ratio of customers to analysts
Basic	X:1
Moderately complex	Y:1
Complex	Z:1

This approach may work moderately well for the startup of a new support center, but in my experience ratios do not accurately predict the needed staffing level. That is why there are no recommendations in the table above.

A more accurate approach to estimating the needed staffing level is based on past history of the number of support requests received, the pattern in which they arrived and how long it takes on average to work them. Using past history as the basis for future projections, the support center can get a good estimate of how many analysts are needed. In order to gather past history, you need to run reports from both the ACD (if available) and the service management system. All ACDs will provide reporting on average handle time (talk time plus after-call work time) and the overall number of calls received, and most will provide a historical view of when the calls arrived (according to the hour of the day and the day of the week). The service management system is needed to account for electronic support requests, or for all support requests if there is no ACD. There are several ways to project headcount requirements once you gather this information, which we will explore in a moment.

Startup support centers and centers that are going to support a new product are at a disadvantage in using this method, which is why a straightforward ratio-based estimate is appealing in these situations. However, projecting an estimate of calling patterns is far more accurate than using a ratio model, even though it takes more effort. With the use of a spreadsheet, you can estimate the calling or contact patterns of your customers. Granted, it is based on educated guessing, which is the best you can do with no prior history to use.

Projecting an estimate of calling patterns is far more accurate than using a ratio model.

Let us take a scenario in which a support center is anticipating the release of a new product to its customers. The release schedule projects that one-fourth of the customers will receive the new product every month. In addition, the support center estimates that the new customers will contact the support center on average three times a month for the first month after release, once the next month and then once every three months thereafter. This part is an educated guess. Your spreadsheet might look like the one on page 224.

If this were a new release for an existing support center, you would add these anticipated contacts to the normal contact projection numbers for those months. If the support center were new, obviously you would use these projections for launch.

Once you have the number of contacts anticipated and the average handle time for the contacts, you now have a number of methods to choose from for calculating needed headcount. There are several inexpensive but effective tools available on the internet that use Erlang calculations (see Support Handling Methods for a discussion on Erlang calculations) to estimate needed staffing levels. Please see www.krconsulting.com for an up-to-date list of possible vendors. Alternatively, read on to learn about a spreadsheet-based tool that can help you estimate staffing levels.

Contact Pattern Estimate for Release of Product 123

Assumptions: a. 1,000 customers in total
b. 250 customers receive release each month
c. Contact pattern: Customers call/contact support 3 times in first month, once the following month and once every 3 months thereafter
d. Average handle time of the calls will be 15 minutes

	Contact pattern: month 1		Contact pattern: month 2		Contact pattern: month 3		
	Customers receiving product	Estimated calls	Customers in month 2	Estimated calls	Customers in month 3	Estimated calls	Total additional calls
Month 1	250	750	0	0	0	0	750
Month 2	250	750	250	250	0	0	1,000
Month 3	250	750	250	250	250	83	1,083
Month 4	250	750	250	250	500	167	1,167
Month 5	0		250	250	750	250	500
Month 6	0		0	0	1,000	333	333
etc.							etc.

Gross Staffing Calculations

One low-cost but accurate way to estimate the number of analysts needed is to use a spreadsheet-based gross staffing calculation. This tool can be helpful to support managers who may have estimated their needed headcount on anecdotal information such as the observation that customers are waiting a longer time than before, or that the new release of the software next quarter is going to increase the volume of calls. The gross staffing calculator is invaluable in these situations.

There are several data elements that you will need to gather in order to run this calculation. The inputs into this calculation are:

- Number of contacts expected or received, separated by medium such as phone or electronic request.
- Percentage of contacts that are escalated to second-level within the support center.
- Average handle time for each time of contact, at both first- and second-level within the support center.

- Amount of time in an average analyst's year that is not devoted to answering incoming contacts (shrinkage).

The calculation multiplies the average handle time by the number of expected support requests to come up with a gross work time, and then divides it by the available hours in an average analyst's year to find needed headcount.

Your service management system or ACD, or a combination of both, should be able to help you calculate the average handle time for all contacts.

On the next page is an example of the gross staffing calculator. The first two sections calculate the amount of work expected at both first and second levels within the support center. Second-level calculations are based on a percentage of the first-level contacts, but you can modify this spreadsheet tool to accommodate a different relationship between first- and second-level support requests.

The third section calculates the net number of hours in a year that an analyst can devote to handling support requests. It starts with 2,080 hours, which is the total theoretical working hours in a year, assuming 40 hours a week is multiplied by 52 weeks. Of course, no one works 2,080 hours because we all take vacation and sick time. There are other shrinkage activities that must be subtracted from the potential hours available, such as meetings, training, and research or project time. The net of shrinkage hours produces the potential direct labor hours available in a year.

The fourth section takes the potential direct labor hours and applies an occupancy percentage to the hours. The occupancy percentage, which averages 70 percent in a small to medium-sized support center, represents the percentage of scheduled on-queue time that analysts are handling customer contacts. The other 30 percent of the time, they are waiting for the next support request or talking with their neighbor in-between calls. If your support

Gross Staffing Calculation

1. Direct labor requirements for processing tickets at first-level per month		
Submission method	Phone	Email
# of incoming contacts per month	2,544	823
Average handle time in minutes (talk plus work time)	10	13
Percentage of incoming contacts that require follow-up outbound calls/emails	20.00%	60.00%
Average handle time in minutes (talk plus work time) for follow-up outbound contacts	8	10
Total required time (mins per month)	**45,147.4**	
2. Direct labor requirements for resolving tickets at second-level per month		
Submission method	Phone	Email
Percentage of contacts escalated to second-level	25%	35%
Average time to resolve	10	10
Total direct labor required (mins per month)	**9,240.5**	
Total direct labor required (hrs/month)	**906.465**	
3. Number of potential direct labor hours available		
Hours per week per agent	40	
Number of weeks per year	52	
Theoretical hours/year available	2,080	
Less other time requirements (shrinkage)		
Company holidays (10 days/year)	80	
Vacations (10 days/year)	80	
Sick time (5 days/year)	40	
Training (10 days/year)	80	
Research time (10 hours/week@45 weeks)	450	
Meetings (1 hour/week @ 45 weeks)	45	
Admin time: breaks, etc. (.5 hour/day@45 weeks)	112.5	
Total potential hours per agent per year	**1,192.5**	
4. Actual # of direct labor hours available		
Potential hours available	1,192.5	
X occupancy percentage	70%	
Direct labor hours available/agent/year	834.75	
Monthly direct labor hours available/agent	**69.5625**	
5. Gross staffing level		
Total hours required	906.465	
Divided by actual hrs available/agent	69.6	
# agents required	**13.0**	
Plus management and support staff		
# of managers/supervisors	1	
# of trainers	0.5	
# of knowledge managers	0.5	
Other administrative staff	1	
Total support center staffing:	**16.0**	

analysts handle emails in-between calls, then your occupancy could be 90 percent or above. If occupancy is above 90 percent, the support center is in danger of high attrition. Think about it — 90 percent occupancy allows only six minutes per hour of down time between serving customers. This is an influential number in the calculation, so carefully consider your entry for occupancy.

In the fifth section of the calculator, the total work hours required is divided by the actual hours available per agent, which produces a total number of analysts required. The last section incorporates the additional management and support staff needed to produce the final headcount requirement.

A copy of the gross staffing calculator spreadsheet is included in the accompanying CD. To purchase the CD, see information at the end of this book.

Scheduling

So now we have an estimate of how many analysts are needed to staff the support center. Next, we need to schedule the analysts so the right number is available to handle support requests when they arrive. The motto for workforce management (the process of projecting needed headcount and creating schedules) is to have the optimum number of people in place at the right time to handle contacts.

> **Schedule the analysts so the right number is available to handle support requests when they arrive.**

Mid-sized and larger support centers calculate their schedules by projecting the anticipated call/contact arrival patterns or how many contacts they expect to receive each hour of the week, and then calculating how many analysts are needed to handle that volume. In a small center, a more static approach can be sufficient. In any case, knowing your peak contact volume times is critical to scheduling properly.

To discern your peak contact volume times, you can analyze your contact arrival pattern by graphing it in two ways, intra-day and weekly:

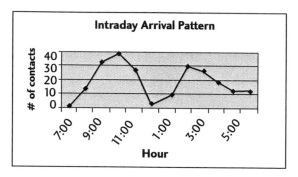

This arrival pattern is often seen in internal support centers that serve customers in the same time zone. You can see that there is a peak mid-morning and mid-afternoon, corresponding to when customers most frequently contact the support center. There is a valley during lunchtime. If the support center serves customers across different time zones, the peaks and valleys may be less pronounced, producing a steadier arrival pattern.

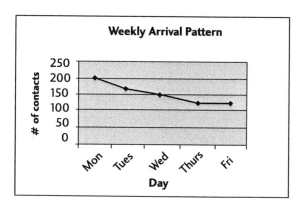

This weekly arrival pattern is typical of an internal support center where Monday is the busiest day, and Monday morning is the busiest half-day. Your support center may deviate from this pattern for any number of reasons. If Mondays are the busiest day, the astute support center supervisor will make sure that all analysts are scheduled to work the phones all day on Monday, and all off-phone activity is scheduled for other days. The supervisor may even wish to have overlapping shifts that day; for example, all analysts who work 4/10 shifts are scheduled to work on Monday to staff for higher volumes that day.

For a small center, the following schedule works well. This approach acknowledges that Mondays are busiest but does not staff for hourly arrival patterns. Rather, it staffs in morning and afternoon time blocks.

XYZ Support Center Schedule

	Monday			Tuesday			Wednesday			Thursday			Friday		
7:00	A			A			A			A			A		
8:00	A	B	C	A	B	C	A	B	C	A	B	C	A	B	C
9:00	A	B	C	A	B	C	A	B	C	A	B	C	A	B	C
10:00	A	B	C	A	B	C	A	B	C	A	B	C	A	B	C
11:00	A	B	C	A	B	C	A	B	C	A	B	C	A	B	C
12:00	A	B	C	A	B	C	A	B	C	A	B	C	A	B	C
1:00	A	B	C	A	B	C	A	B	C	A	B	C	A	B	C
2:00	A	B	C	A	B	C	A	B	C	A	B	C	A	B	C
3:00	A	B	C	A	B	C	A	B	C	A	B	C	A	B	C
4:00	A	B	C	A	B	C	A	B	C	A	B	C	A	B	C
5:00		B	C		B	C		B	C		B	C		B	C

Legend: Phones, emails
Desk side/projects
Lunch
Meetings
A,B,C represent the three support center analysts

Notice first that every analyst is scheduled for phone support on Monday morning – the "all hands on deck" approach to handling the high volume of expected calls. Notice also that each analyst is scheduled for off-phone times twice a week. In this internal support center, analysts are scheduled to provide desk-side support during those times. This offers the analysts job diversity and the ability to get out of the center and make face-to-face contact with customers. It also gives them time to research issues from previous support requests, make proactive calls to customers and do project work.

If a formal approach to scheduling is anathema to your small support center, you may choose the buddy approach to scheduling breaks and lunch times. Each support analyst is paired with a buddy and told that only one buddy can be at lunch or on break at the same time. This ensures that only half of your support center will be absent at any one time and creates accountability between the team members. A white board that lists all the analysts and where they are (i.e.: lunch or break) at the present time helps with accountability. Analysts should sign in and out so that everyone can see where they are. Even if you implement the buddy approach, be sure to schedule times for off-phone activities during the week.

For support centers bigger than about 10 analysts, a more formal approach to scheduling is appropriate. Each support center has a contact arrival pattern that is unique. The first step in creating a schedule is to determine the historical contact arrival pattern for each hour the support center is open. This is gathered from the ACD if all your contacts are phone-based, from a combination of the ACD and service management system if you take a combination of phone- and electronic-based requests, or from the service management system if you take only electronic requests. This may take some digging, as service management systems are not typically set up to report this. What makes it challenging is that the objective is to create an average hourly arrival pattern, so you may need to take several sample weeks' data and average them. What you are seeking is a matrix that shows contacts per hour, like this:

Weekly Average Contact Arrival Volumes

	Monday	Tuesday	Wednesday	Thursday	Friday
7:00	7	5	5	3	3
7:30	8	7	10	8	6
8:00	19	10	10	17	15
8:30	20	14	14	12	14
9:00	20	14	14	20	16
9:30	25	13	13	22	17
10:00	23	16	17	20	18
10:30	20	17	17	25	17
11:00	21	22	17	25	17
11:30	15	10	7	8	13
12:00	14	9	8	8	13
12:30	10	9	9	10	11
1:00	10	10	9	10	11
1:30	17	14	15	17	10
2:00	20	15	15	21	10
2:30	16	15	12	21	8
3:00	19	20	17	25	9
3:30	18	19	13	20	9
4:00	18	20	14	16	3
4:30	17	17	10	14	2
5:00	8	8	10	14	2
5:30	7	7	5	10	1
Total:	**352**	**291**	**261**	**346**	**225**
Weekly total:					**1475**

If your contact arrivals patterns are static, you can stop there. This is the point where it is prudent to purchase one of the inexpensive scheduling tools available online. These tools will create schedules for your analysts that include staggered shifts, lunches, breaks and on- and off-phone times. The time saved by these inexpensive tools more than compensates for the dollars invested in them.

A best practice in support centers is to schedule time off the phones every day or several times during the week for each analyst. The time off the phone should be devoted to researching open support requests, training, working on knowledge solutions or performing additional roles. If support analysts do not have a formal off-phone time during their day, they take time in-between calls (regardless of the current phone volume) to research an issue and get back to the customer. However, if you create regularly scheduled off-phone time for the analysts, they will save their research work and do it during that time. This can actually make your support center more productive, because the analysts are focused on answering the phones or emails during their "on-queue" time, rather than taking time between calls to follow up with a previous customer. Off-phone times are scheduled during historically low call volume times or when shifts overlap and there are more people in the support center than needed for expected volumes. A good way to start is to schedule 30 minutes a day for everyone, then increase the off-phone time as team members advance through the ranks of the career ladder. Perhaps an analyst I has 30 minutes off-phone daily, and others have more. The amount of off-queue time that is right for your center is dependent on the nature of the support provided and the support request handling method chosen.

If support analysts do not have a formal off-phone time during their day, they take time in-between calls.

In a support center that I ran in which we followed the touch and hold method, I offered a choice to the analysts: either have two hours daily off the phones or one day a week off the phones. The analysts chose one day a week, reasoning that they could accomplish more in one eight-hour day of uninterrupted time than in 10 hours spread out over a week. This worked for our group for a time while volumes were relatively low, but we had to change it to the every-day plan as volumes increased and we discovered that customers were waiting too long for callbacks on their unresolved support requests. This was because the analysts had to wait for their once-a-week day off to perform their research.

Electronic Requests

Staffing for electronic requests deserves special consideration. Electronic requests are requests received either via email or through a web-based entry form. In either case, these requests are asynchronous (delayed response) support requests, and they can pose some staffing challenges, especially if the support center offers this medium in addition to phone support. Some support centers provide only electronic support, so these considerations are not a concern to them.

There are three ways you might staff to handle electronic support requests:

1. Dedicated teams
2. Functional time blocks
3. Between calls

Unless you have a multi-media distribution system that automatically assigns electronic requests to individuals the way an ACD distributes calls to the next available agent, you probably need to use some sort of dispatch support request handling method. (Please refer to Chapter Four: Support Request Handling Methods for a discussion of the dispatch method.) The three ways can be summarized as follows on page 234.

The coordinator who distributes the incoming electronic support requests may be the support center manager, a senior analyst or some other person designated to assign incoming support requests to the proper person. In order to properly assign and distribute the support requests correctly and effectively, this person needs to be knowledgeable of the skills each analyst possesses, of each person's existing workload and of the priority of the request.

Electronic Support Request Handling

Handling model	Dedicated teams	Functional time blocks	Between calls
Description	Analysts are hired to do email or phone support only. Unless there is a multi-media distribution system, electronic requests are distributed by a coordinator.	Analysts are scheduled for email time blocks and phone time blocks during the week. Unless there is only one person, electronic requests are distributed by a coordinator.	Analysts respond to email between calls. A coordinator distributes electronic requests.
Benefits	Hiring made easy. Expert skills. Lowest AHT.	Gives reps job diversity, time off phones. Keeps backlog down and response time up.	Increases utilization.
Drawbacks	Possibility of "small queue" syndrome; can be inefficient. No job diversity or skills enhancement.	Possibility of "small queue" syndrome; can be inefficient. Not everyone can write well – need training.	Can be stressful. Can divert attention from answering phone calls, decreasing service levels.
Applications	Usually seen only in large support centers.	Common in both small and medium support centers.	Best used when phone volume is light, e.g.; night shift.

Best Practices – Staffing and Scheduling

1. Support centers use either a gross staffing model or Erlang-based calculators to determine how many analysts are needed.

2. Create schedules for analysts that allow time for off-phone activities such as project-related work or roles, job-shadowing or desk-side support (in internal centers).

3. Small support centers should create simple schedules and may use the buddy method for scheduling breaks and lunches. Mid-sized centers need to be more formal in their schedules and should use an inexpensive scheduling tool to create them.

4. Unless electronic support requests are distributed automatically to analysts, they need special considerations to ensure that these requests are responded to in a timely manner.

## CHAPTER FIFTEEN

Change Management and the Product Development Life Cycle

IN AN INTERNAL SUPPORT CENTER, its interface with development is most often mediated through change management, the process that guides the organization in approving and implementing changes to the IT infrastructure. ITIL defines the elements of an excellent change management process, and we will explore some of those elements as they pertain to the smaller support center and smaller IT shop. External support centers follow many of the best practices in change management, but because the company is usually dedicated to developing, selling and supporting its own product, there is a market need to include the support center's viewpoint at multiple points in the product development process. We will examine separately change management for IT organizations and the product development life cycle for high-tech companies.

Change Management and Its Importance to IT

In IT organizations, a change is defined as a modification or alteration to the status of a software application, network functionality or hardware-related tool. Changes can be large or routine, such as setting up a computer for a new hire. (Large changes, or an aggregate of smaller changes, form a release. Release management, another ITIL process that is closely related to change management, is not dealt with in this book.) Changes can be initiated by support requests received at the support center, by business users requesting new technology tools or by IT management as it plans for and responds to the business needs of the organization.

A formal and effective change management process enables the

A solid change management process can dramatically reduce costs.

IT organization to reduce or eliminate disruptions to IT operations and business activities. Change management ensures that all parties are properly notified of the change, that the risks inherent in the change have been assessed and that a back-out plan is in place in case of failure. A solid change management process can dramatically reduce costs by minimizing unplanned downtime, reducing the amount of re-work associated with unsuccessful changes and minimizing calls to the support center.

Change management is one of the most important processes in an IT organization. The negative consequences of a weak or non-existent change management process are legendary. According to industry experts, unauthorized and unplanned changes account for 80 percent of IT downtime. Additionally, 60-80 percent of unplanned changes fail, and more than half of all IT changes are unplanned.

The most obvious symptom of a broken change management process is that the support center hears of changes from customers who report an issue with the change. Not only is it embarrassing to the support center to be informed of an IT change by the customer, but it indicates that changes are not being managed and communicated effectively throughout the organization.

Best Practices in Change Management

Most organizations create a change advisory board (CAB) or change control board (CCB) to manage changes. A change manager, who is responsible for receiving all requests for change (RFC) and coordinating the organization's change process, chairs the CAB. All IT stakeholders have a seat on the CAB, including representatives of affected customer groups, the support center and other IT groups. In many organizations, the CAB meets regularly to review, prioritize and schedule RFCs. Additionally, the CAB can conduct its work electronically via email.

Even in small IT organizations, it is not advisable that the support manager assume the responsibilities of the change manager. An application analyst or developer should assume this role, as it requires a close interface to those functions.

By categorizing changes to the infrastructure, the IT organization can prioritize and coordinate its response to change. There are two major types of changes: planned and unplanned. A sub-set of the CAB can be designated to deal with emergency RFCs, which are defined as critical changes that must be made quickly due to a problem that has major impact to the customer base.

Standard changes are those that are pre-authorized by the CAB to be resolved by the support center using standard processes. Examples of standard changes are password resets, moves/adds/changes or routine swapping of hardware parts. It makes sense for the CAB to delegate responsibility for standard changes to the support center. Part of the support center's responsibilities in performing these changes is to inform the change manager and to update the configuration management database.

> **Standard changes are those that are pre-authorized by the CAB.**

Planned Changes

Severity of change	Standard	Minor	Significant	Major
Description	Tasks are well-known and solutions are proven and can be delegated to IT organizations such as the support center.	Minor or repetitive changes considered part of the normal workflow.	Small changes that have a documented and proven implementation process.	Changes that may affect multiple applications across multiple departments.
Impact on operations	No affect on operations.	No affect on the customer's business.	Little impact to the customer's business.	Significant impact to customer's business.
Notification to customer	None	None	IT informs customer at least 3 days in advance of the outage.	IT informs the customer at least 5 days before the outage, with a reminder on the day of the outage.
Process	Responsible group documents change; updates CMDB.	Under change control	Under change control	Under change control
Examples	User is promoted and needs access to additional applications; MACs.	Add additional jobs to backup schedule.	Server settings or configuration changes.	Major network changes or outages. Conversions. PBX upgrade. Major office moves.

Unplanned Changes

Severity of change	Critical (after hours)	Emergency (during business hours)
Description	Changes that must be performed in order to correct a faulty IT service.	Changes that must be performed in order to correct a faulty IT service.
Impact on operations	Major impact on some customers' business.	Major impact on customer's business. Impact to business requires immediate resolution.
Notification to customer	Information technology advises customer as soon as possible after knowing such a change is required.	Service desk reactively informs customer as soon as a problem is known. Information technology informs customer after resolution of problem.
Examples	Outage	Outage

One important step in planning changes is to create a rollback or regression plan if the change is unsuccessful. Even small IT organizations should undertake this important discipline. A rollback plan restores the infrastructure to its previous state; for example, in a software upgrade the rollback plan would be to re-install the previous software version. Failing to plan a back-out strategy can be costly to the organization.

The CAB and change manager should prepare and publish a calendar of planned changes, often called a forward schedule of changes (FSC). This calendar projects the times of each change and is a vehicle for communication of the changes. The support center's representative to the CAB should regularly review the FSC with the support center so planned changes are not a surprise.

Convincing all IT stakeholders to follow one standardized process for change can be challenging. Some ways to ensure compliance with change management procedures include:

- Oversight of change management compliance by IT executives who impose consequences for non-compliance with established procedures.
- A regular review of unsuccessful changes (sometimes called post-mortems) that identify the root causes of the failure.
- Training on change management procedures for all IT individuals.

Flowcharts for the change management process are included on the companion CD, which can be ordered from KR Consulting. See the end of this book for details.

The Support Center's Role in Change Management

The support center is an important player in the change management process. The support center should:

- **Record request for changes.**

  The support center often receives requests for changes from the user community. It is the support center's job to record those requests and notify change management of them.

- **Communicate the schedule of changes to the user community.**

  It is the support center's duty to inform the users of changes. This might be accomplished by broadcasting emails to the company that tell of changes taking place over the weekend. Changes could also be communicated through an IT e-newsletter.

- **Participate in the change advisory board.**

  The support center should be represented on the CAB. That representative should report to the entire support center with news and upcoming events.

- **Prepare for the change.**

  The support center will receive any incidents caused by the change. Training, documentation and knowledge solutions should be created to ease the implementation of the change and prepare the support center for the change.

- **Implement standard changes.**

  The support center should be empowered to implement pre-approved, standard changes. Support center personnel should record those changes so they can be reported to change management.

- **Recording incidents related to all changes.**

  This is the job of the support center.

- **Report to upper management.**

  Once the incidents are recorded, the support center reports the number and nature of incidents received.

- **Assess the customer's satisfaction with changes.**

  The support center should be the body that conducts

event-driven and one-time surveys to measure customer satisfaction with changes.

Change Reviews

As mentioned above, all changes, not just unsuccessful ones, should be reviewed either to celebrate success in order to duplicate them, or to identify process improvements. Here are some questions that might be used in a change review session.

- Did the change accomplish its goal?
- If it was unsuccessful, why?
  o Root cause analysis – Why was it unsuccessful?
- Fishbone diagram, five why's, other techniques.
- Was the regression plan invoked successfully?
- What were the number and nature of incidents related to the change?
- Were there unexpected consequences of the change?
- Was it accomplished within budget?
- What can we do better next time?
  o How can we ensure that it is done?

Product Development Life Cycle (for External Support Centers)

In a high-tech company, the support center must be closely involved in the product development cycle. The benefits are three-fold:

1. Products that better meet the needs of the customers (as opposed to what is technically possible).
2. Lower overall support costs.
3. More new product sales (because the product meets the customer's needs).

Support should be involved in every phase of the development life cycle, with the exception of programming. The development life cycle commonly looks like this:

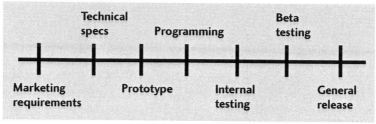

Development Life Cycle

In many companies, approval is needed from sales, marketing and support at checkpoints during each phase, above. However, it is more than just a rubber-stamping of development's efforts. It starts with support regularly creating reports of the feedback it receives from customers regarding the product. This feedback is collected through customer satisfaction surveys, conversations with customers, and information received during onsite installations and training. The support center summarizes and categorizes the feedback and indicates the importance of each category.

Next, the support liaison meets with the product manager to discuss what is included in the marketing requirements document. Concurrently, a defect or change board composed of analysts from support, product marketing, development and occasionally sales meets regularly with the product manager to discuss and jointly prioritize defect reports. This body may decide that a patch release is needed to consolidate a number of one-off patches that development has created. The defect board feeds prioritized defects into the marketing requirements document. The marketing requirements document is approved by sales, support and marketing.

The developers then create a functional specification and prototypes of the new product. Again, approval is necessary for advancement to the next stage.

The support center should be responsible for testing the product after QA has performed unit testing. Involving the support center in testing the software or product release has two benefits:

1. The support analysts have a chance to become familiar with the software release.
2. Support analysts understand exactly how customers use the software and can test it well.

Defects found at this point should be presented to the defect board, which prioritizes and makes the decision about delaying the release or not.

The support center should also be responsible for supporting the beta test, and the number of customers chosen to test the software should be proportional to the scope of the release and represent a variety of environments. The results of beta testing are again presented to the defect board for prioritization of defects found. A best practice is an executive commitment to fix all critical known defects before release, even if it will delay the release date.

> **The support center should also be responsible for supporting the beta test.**

In the meantime, the support center must document its support readiness plan. This project plan should include all the tasks needed to get the support center ready to support the new product. Elements in the support readiness plan might include:

- Plans for internal testing.
- Plans for beta testing.
- Plans to update the knowledge base with information learned during beta testing.
- New support processes needed to support the new software (for example, how to handle clients who ask for a software CD when they can download it from the FTP site themselves).

- Plans for creating internal training documentation and updating new hire training.
- Plans for delivering training to the support center.
- Plans for creating customer training.
- Plans for delivering customer training.

The support readiness plan can be as simple as a document listing the tasks, or as complex as a Microsoft Project plan with dependencies and a critical path.

Enhancements Requests and Defect Tracking

The support center is often the first to hear of enhancement requests and defects. It is important that the support center has a way to record both enhancement requests and defects, and that they are tracked using a closed-loop process. Most support centers have a way to convert a support request record to a defect record, if only through re-entering information into product development's defect tracking system.

Many support centers require that a product specialist or development liaison approve defect reports; this practice ensures that someone who has deep understanding of the product is entering defect records. It also helps to reduce duplicate entry of defects. What is important is to keep track of the number of support requests related to a defect. This is often handled by creating a parent-and-child relationship between a defect record and the support requests, if they are in the same database. Alternatively, the support center might enter the defect record number into the support request record to create a link, like this simulated support request screen:

Keep track of the number of support requests related to a defect.

The defect number is recorded in the support request record. This enables the support center to report on the number of support

Record number: b97867564

Customer:	Allied Metal	**Customer #**	123456b7
Contact:	Jane Doe	**Products:**	AP
Address:	1234 Main Street		AR
City:	Indianapolis		GL
State:	IN		
Zip:	46010		
Tel:	317-123-4567		

Category:	Software	**Defect #:**	3211507
Type:	GL	**Approved:**	Jay
Item:	Reports	**Enhancement #:**	

Short description: Proforma budget report prints unreadable

Long description:
Customer says she's running the proforma budget from the GL, and is getting unreadable characters in the far right column. This just started happening since she installed the new release.

Support Request Screen

requests recorded against this defect. Support representatives bring reports that show the number of calls received on each defect to the defect review meeting. This information helps prioritize defects.

Some support centers actually quantify the cost of a defect. This is easy to do if you have a report of the number of support requests received on a defect. To estimate the support cost of a defect, multiply the average cost per support request (see Chapter One: Strategic Leadership for instructions on how to calculate this figure) by the number of support requests received on a defect. This is a conservative figure because it does not include costs of development's time to fix the defect, the financial effect on the customer or the damage to the company's reputation if the defect is critical.

Many companies offer customers a form on the support web site for entering enhancement requests, which are usually directed toward product marketing personnel. Support analysts should also have the opportunity to record enhancement requests into a database that is shared with product marketing.

For both enhancement requests and defects, a best practice is to proactively notify customers who have reported them when the status of the record changes. For example, if a defect record's status changes from "pending" to "approved for release," a notification should be sent to all the customers who reported the defect that product development will be working on it and the fix will be in the next release. This assumes integration between the defect tracking system and the service management system, in order to find the customers who have reported the defect. Alternatively, some support centers expect their development liaisons to identify the customers who reported the defect and notify them (usually through email) that the defect is scheduled to be fixed in an upcoming release.

Best Practices – Change Management

1. Establish change processes and ensure that all employees understand the need for them and the consequences of non-compliance with them.
2. A support center representative sits on the change advisory board (CAB).
3. A calendar of planned changes is published and shared with the support center.
4. A back-out or regression plan is included in all planned changes.
5. All changes are reviewed using a post-mortem change review form.

Best Practices — Product Development Life Cycle

1. The support center is involved in each phase of the product development cycle.
2. During the marketing requirements phase, the support center communicates the product feedback it gathers and presents it to product marketing and development.
3. The support center should test new releases internally and be involved in the customer beta testing program.
4. The support center should create a support readiness plan prior to product release.
5. The support center should approve the release of a new product.
6. Executives should commit to releasing products only when all critical known defects are corrected.
7. The support center should proactively notify customers of the status of their enhancement request or defect report.

Appendices

Appendix A: Call Evaluation Legend

Here is a description of each item on the call evaluation form.

1. Did the analyst use the standard greeting?
Description:

A consistent greeting portrays the professionalism of the support center. The greeting has several elements:

- Identify the department, company or support center.
- Give the caller your (the analyst's) name.
- Request the information needed first (this could be simply "How can I help you?"). For other centers, it helps to request the identifier of the caller in order to expedite retrieving the customer's record. This practice should be headlined in the ACD greeting, as in "In order to serve you more quickly, please have your customer number ready for the analyst."

A smile on the face results in a pleasant, friendly voice that sets the tone for the rest of the interaction.

Note: Only the greeting is a script, not suggested wording. Consistency is needed to create a positive, professional image of the support center.

Wording:

"ABC customer support, this is {analyst's name}, may I please have your customer number?"

2. Did the analyst actively listen to the customer without interrupting?
Description:

Completing other tasks and taking a deep breath before answering the phone helps you focus on the caller. Remove all distractions.

Let the caller complete a thought or sentence without interrupting. Use comforting mutterings to communicate to the caller you are listening.

Suggested wording:

Comforting mutterings: "Un huh; I see; yes, go on; hmm; oh"

3. Did the analyst paraphrase and confirm the problem description?

Description:

Paraphrasing is re-stating the problem in your own words in order to confirm the problem. This is an important step to ensure that you solve the right problem, rather than an assumed problem. Repeating verbatim what the customer says may be helpful when talking to technically unsophisticated customers or if you are unsure of the problem. When repeating the terminology used by an unsophisticated customer, you can gently educate the customer on the proper phrases to use. Be careful of the tone of voice when offering an alternative term. Any condescension in the voice can turn a contented customer into an angry one – or one that will never call back.

Suggested wording:

"So if I'm hearing you correctly, you are having trouble accessing the network printer from your workstation. Do I have that right?"

OR

"I understand you to say that the TV screen on your desk is flickering. The TV screen can also be called a monitor. Whatever we call it, it's not working properly – is that correct?"

4. Did the analyst ask appropriate questions to properly identify the problem?

Description:

The problem description has two parts: an identification of what object is having the problem and a description of what exactly is wrong with the object. A combination of open-ended and closed-ended questions may be needed to pin down the problem.

Suggested wording:

"What exactly is having the problem?" (closed-ended question) "Is it the printer or the computer that is making a funny noise?" (closed-ended question) "Can you describe what the noise sounds like?" (open-ended question)

5. **Did the analyst ask appropriate questions to explore conditions in order to troubleshoot?**

Description:

Troubleshooting questions explore the conditions of the problem and are the way an analyst searches for clues to what is wrong and how to fix it. What, where, when and how questions help you gather clues and make educated guesses about the root cause of the problem. Comparison questions that ask what or where the problem is not happening also help pinpoint the problem.

Suggested wording:

"When did the noise start?" "What happens when the noise starts?" "Where does it seem to come from?" "How many of the computers in your office have this problem?" "What computers are NOT having the problem?"

6. **Did the analyst effectively use his resources to research possible solutions?**

Description:

As a support analyst, you have several resources at your disposal, all of which are searchable from the Intranet: the knowledge base, previous solutions posted to the service management system, product manuals and the defects database. After checking these resources, if you are still at a loss, contact the senior analyst group via IM or the senior line. The senior analyst can help you troubleshoot and identify a solution. If you referred to the knowledge base, make a link in the support request record to the solution you accessed.

Suggested wording:

"I know we've come across that situation before. Please bear with me while I check my online resources to make sure the answer I give you is 100 percent accurate."

OR

"I think I know how to solve this, but I need to check with the expert in this area to confirm my assessment. Can you please hold for a moment while I do that?"

7. Did the analyst try to replicate the customer's problem?
Description:

As a troubleshooting step, it may be necessary to attempt to replicate the customer's problem on your machine. Sometimes it is easy to do this while the customer is on the phone; other times, you may have to call the customer back after re-creating the situation on the analyst's equipment.

Suggested wording:

"Could you please walk me through what you entered into the A13 screen? I'd like to see if the same thing happens on my machine."

8. Did the analyst follow escalation guidelines and escalate when appropriate?
Description:

In order to focus on answering incoming calls within the service level requirements, the first-level analyst should contact his senior analyst if the call time has extended beyond 15 minutes. If the analyst believes that he can resolve the support request within five more minutes, the senior will allow the analyst to continue. Otherwise, the senior will take over the call.

Suggested wording:

"Can I put you on hold while I contact my senior analyst about this support request?" (Wait for answer) "Great, please hold."

9. **Did the analyst educate the customer on how to use the self-service knowledge base?**

Description:

Mention the existence of the online knowledge base for the customer's future use. This encourages self-reliance in the customer and may be the first time the customer has learned about this alternative support method. If the customer is willing, you can show her how to access the knowledge base by connecting to her computer by remote control, or you can describe step-by-step how to access the knowledge base. This investment of time can save a future call to support.

Suggested wording:

"Did you know that this resolution is in our online knowledge base? Would you like me to show you how to access it? It is rather fun to know that you can solve your own problem sometimes. You can always call us for help, but this might be a good alternative, especially when we're busy."

10. **Did the analyst state the resolution plan in a clear manner?**

Description:

Give the customer an overview of the resolution before jumping into the resolution steps. When you get the customer's agreement (called a verbal contract) to proceed, you create a partnership between you and the customer. The customer is more likely to work with you.

Suggested wording:

"What we're going to do is restore your Internet connection by powering down your modem and router, then restarting. Can I walk you through those steps right now?"

11. Did the analyst walk the customer through the steps to solve the problem?

Description:

Clearly describe the steps to solve the problem and patiently walk the customer through each step.

Suggested wording:

"Let's start with the first step. Do you know where the power switch is on your modem? Great, could you turn it off for me and make sure that all the lights go off?"

12. Did the analyst test the solution presented and take action?

Description:

After walking the customer through the resolution steps, take the time to ensure that the solution fixed the problem. You can do this by asking the customer to try to complete the task that she was prevented from doing.

Suggested wording:

"OK, could you try turning on your monitor now to see if it still flickers?"

13. Did the analyst give the support request record number to the customer?

Description:

In all calls, give the customer the case number to encourage the customer to look it up in the online case management system. In the case of an escalated call, give the case number to help the customer check on its status in the future.

Suggested wording:

"I'd like to give you the case number of this call, just in case you'd like to look it up in our online case management tool. You may come across this issue again, and the steps we took will be documented in this case to remind you what to do. Do you have a pencil? The case number is 12345."

OR

"I need to escalate this case to an expert in this area. That person will be contacting you within eight business hours. Here's your case number so you can track its status in our online case management tool. Are you ready for that number? The case number is 12345."

14. Did the analyst use the standard close?

Description:

A consistent closing portrays the professionalism of the group. The closing should include an offer to help with another issue, an expression of thanks for calling and encouragement to call again.

Suggested wording:

"Is there anything else I can help you with today? Well, thank you for calling, and don't hesitate to call us again. Goodbye."

15. Did the analyst instill confidence in the caller?

Description:

After confirming the problem statement, assure the customer that you can help. This simple statement builds confidence in your ability and willingness to help. It helps set up a partnership with the customer.

Suggested wording:

"I can help you with that" or "I'd be glad to help you with that today."

16. Did the analyst transfer the call according to guidelines?

Description:

If a customer needs to be transferred, for whatever reason, put the customer on hold, dial the phone number of the employee you need and wait for that person to answer. Explain the situation to your colleague, then conference in the customer. This ensures that the customer does not have to explain the situation again to the new analyst. This is a warm transfer.

Suggested wording:

"I'd like to transfer you to an expert in this area who can help you with this problem. If that's OK, can you please hold for a moment while I call that person?" {Wait for agreement}

"Thanks for holding. I have {analyst's name} on the phone now, and I've explained your problem to her. She's going to help you from here. Thanks for calling."

17. Did the analyst use the client's name at least once?

Description:

Use the customer's name at least once during the call. This personalizes the encounter and lets a customer know you care enough to remember his or her name. It is convenient to use the name right after getting the customer's name but OK to use at other times during the call. Excessive use of the customer's name (more than once or twice per call) is not recommended.

Suggested wording:

"Thank you, {first name}." or "Thank you, Dr./Ms./Mr. {last name}. {Use first or last names according to your customer's status and your support center's practices.}

18. Did the analyst headline the need to put the customer on hold and control hold time?

Description:

If there is a need to put a customer on hold, the best way is to ask the customer for permission, wait for an answer and then put her on hold. Being put on hold is frustrating to a customer because she only has two choices: to hang up and call back or to hold without knowing when the analyst will come back on the line. About two minutes is the maximum time a customer should be put on hold. At that time, a best practice is to come back on the line and offer to call the customer back.

Suggested wording:

"I need to confirm that information for you. Can I put you on hold while I call someone, or would you rather I call you back? {Wait for answer} Great, one moment please."

OR

"I need to look up that information for you. Can I put you on hold while I do that? {Wait for answer} Thanks, I'll be right back." {After two minutes of hold time} "Hi {customer's name}, I know you've been holding for a few moments, and it's taking me longer than I thought to find that information. Would you like to continue to hold, or should I call you back?"

19. If the caller was angry or emotional, did the analyst handle it appropriately?

Description:

Listening well is the first step in handling an angry customer. Do not interrupt, and let the customer vent. Use comforting mutterings to let the customer know you are paying attention. If the customer is irritated, a light tone of voice with a self-deprecating phrase can be effective. Empathy absorbs emotion. If a caller is emotional at all, empathize. If you ignore the emotion, the customer will feel disrespected and will be difficult to work with. If there is even a remote possibility that your company made a mistake in handling the customer, apologize for it. The analyst need not take the blame for the problem, but apologize in a way that shows accountability.

Suggested wording:

Apologies:

"I'm sorry about that. I guess I haven't had enough coffee yet this morning."

OR

"I'm sorry for the confusion. I'll do my best to correct the situation."

OR

"I apologize for this situation. I'll call the shipper to put a trace on that shipment right away."

Empathy statements:

"Gee, that's terrible. I understand how irritating that can be."

OR

"I can see how upset you are."

OR

"It's clear how critical this shipment is to you. I'll do my best to correct the situation."

20. Did the analyst use "we" words instead of "you"?

Description:

Using commands with the word "you" implies an accusation of the customer and creates an adversarial relationship. On the other hand, using the word "we" creates a sense of teamwork and builds rapport with the customer. Statements such as "You should have done this" will generally anger a customer.

Suggested wording:

"Let's see how we can address that issue together."

OR

"Let's try a better way to do that."

~ 260 ~

21. Did the analyst headline what she is doing during silences?
Description:

Headlining lets you tell the customer what you are going to do before you do it. This addresses the customer's need to be aware and helps him understand why there may be silence on the line. For example, if you have to look up something on the network, you would headline to the customer what you are going to do. This prevents the customer from getting anxious and asking, "Are you still there?"

Suggested wording:

"I'm going to take just a moment to look up that information for you."

OR

"Hmm, let me think about this for just a moment."

22. Did the analyst speak with a friendly and polite tone?
Description:

Speak with a varied pitch, rather than a monotone, to convey interest and friendliness. When you enunciate words with a normal tone, rather than by clipping words, you convey a sense of calm. Use polite words such as "please" and "thank you" to express appreciation of and respect to the customer. Use formal words and pronunciations.

23. Did the analyst effectively control the call?
Description:

Control the call by using a customer's name in order to get her attention and by using closed-ended questions to direct the conversation. Elongating the call by using chitchat (conversation that is not on the topic of the call) should be confined to periods when call volume is low and no calls are waiting. Strike a balance between being friendly and verbose. It is possible for an analyst to control a call too tightly, thereby robbing the customer of needed attention or friendliness.

Suggested wording:

"Mr. Smith, what version of the application are you using?"

Appendix B: Examples of Job Descriptions

Associate Customer Support Analyst
XYZ Support Center

The objective of the Associate Customer Support Analyst is to provide customer and technical support through analysis and problem-solving in order to facilitate installation, implementation, maintenance, education and documentation of technical products via a support center environment. Experience with {list technical requirements}. Also important are communication skills for interfacing with clients and working in a close-knit team environment, and organizational ability for multi-tasking.

The Associate Customer Support Analyst will:

- Provide customer and technical support for assigned products through inbound phone requests.
- Independently identify, troubleshoot, document and replicate customer problems and then escalate complex problems in accordance with the escalation plan.
- Track resolution through the problem-solving cycle.
- Keep impacted parties informed of progress and resolution.
- Develop documentation for customer support and problem resolution for the knowledge base.
- Recommend enhancements regarding product, application or documentation.
- Communicate changes or new developments to customers.

Requirements
- Two years' corporate support experience.
- Two-year degree or equivalent technical support experience.
- {List technical requirements, including any certifications.}
- Strong verbal, written and interpersonal communication skills.
- Ability to troubleshoot and resolve problems in a technical

team-oriented environment.

- Ability to demonstrate customer empathy, good customer diplomacy skills and problem ownership.
- Ability to manage multiple tasks and priorities including good time-management skills.

Customer Support Analyst I
XYZ Support Center

The objective of the Customer Support Analyst I is to provide customer and technical support through analysis and problem-solving in order to facilitate installation, implementation, maintenance, education and documentation of technical products via a support center environment. Experience with {list technical requirements} is required for success in this position. In addition, communication skills are important for interfacing with clients and working in a close-knit team environment, and organizational ability is important for multi-tasking.

The Customer Support Analyst I will:

- Provide customer and technical support to customers through inbound phone and email requests.
- Independently identify, troubleshoot, document and replicate customer problems and then escalate complex problems according to escalation procedures.
- Retain ownership of all cases throughout the resolution process.
- Report enhancement requests received from customers regarding hardware, application or documentation.
- Provide input to escalation departments, through proper escalation procedures.
- Communicate bug fixes and new enhancements to customers.

Requirements

- Two years' corporate support experience with the ability to work flexible hours.

- Two-year degree or equivalent software industry experience.
- Excellent customer service skills, as demonstrated by superior call monitoring ratings
- {List technical requirements, including any certifications.}
- Strong verbal, written and interpersonal communication skills.
- Ability to troubleshoot and resolve problems in a technical team-oriented environment.
- Ability to demonstrate customer empathy, good customer diplomacy skills and problem ownership.
- Ability to manage multiple tasks and priorities including good time-management skills.

Customer Support Analyst II
XYZ Support Center

The objective of the Customer Support Analyst II is to provide customer and technical support through analysis and problem-solving in order to facilitate installation, implementation, maintenance, education and documentation of technical products via a support center environment. Experience with {list technical requirements} is required for success in this position. In addition, communication skills are important for interfacing with clients and working in a close-knit team environment, and organizational ability is important for multi-tasking.

The Customer Support Analyst II will:

- Provide customer and technical support to customers through inbound phone and email requests.
- Independently identify, troubleshoot, document and replicate customer problems and then escalate complex problems according to escalation procedures.
- Retain ownership of all cases throughout the resolution process.

- Report enhancement requests received from customers regarding product, application or documentation.
- Provide input to escalation departments, through proper escalation procedures.
- Communicate bug fixes and new enhancements to customers.
- Develop documentation for customer support and problem resolution for tech info and knowledge base.
- Participate in mentoring and training new team members.
- Test new software releases throughout development cycle.
- Assist less experienced team members with troubleshooting customers' problems.
- Serve as backup to Senior Analysts.

Requirements

This position is open only to internal candidates. Requirements for promotion to Customer Support Analyst II include:

- At least six months' experience as Support Analyst I.
- Proven ability to independently resolve customer's problems.
- Excellent customer service skills, as demonstrated by superior call monitoring ratings.
- {List certifications.}
- Demonstrated deep product expertise in one or two product areas.
- Ability to manage time in order to juggle multiple requirements during the work day.
- Ability to train other team members.

Senior Analyst
XYZ Support Center

The objective of the Senior Analyst is to provide technical assistance to both customers and other team members through analysis and problem-solving in order to facilitate installation, implementation, maintenance, education and documentation of technical products via a support center environment. Deep technical knowledge of {list technical requirements} is a requirement for success in this position. In addition, strong interpersonal skills are necessary to interact with both customers and team members.

The Senior Analyst will:

- Assist other team members with escalated support requests, either by coaching the team member, conferencing in the call or by assuming responsibility for the call.
- Document all requests for assistance in a database.
- Act as main point of contact between the support center and application support.
- Review and analyze all tickets before escalating to any group.
- Review all escalations for possible training opportunities.
- Develop and conduct internal ongoing training sessions.
- Work with team supervisor to develop team members' technical abilities.
- Conduct technical ticket reviews for all team members.
- Accept incoming calls only when incoming volumes are critically high.

Requirements

This position is open only to internal candidates. Requirements for promotion to Senior Analyst include:

- At least six months' experience as Support Analyst II.
- Proven ability to independently resolve customers' problems.
- {List certifications.}
- Demonstrated deep product expertise in one or two product areas.
- Ability to manage time in order to juggle multiple requirements during the work day.
- Ability to train and the aptitude for training other team members.

Productivity Specialist
XYZ Support Center

The Productivity Specialist is responsible for the following tasks:

• **Workforce management system:** Perform configuration and customization of the system. Input schedule requirements. Create group and individual schedules. Act as contact person for all analysts regarding scheduling and attendance issues (e.g.: when an analyst is ill, she will call the productivity specialist). Track attendance and tardies; report attendance and tardies to supervisors and management. Calculate projected staffing requirements. Schedule all intra-day off-phone activities. Monitor support center's intra-day service level compliance, and work with supervisors when deviations occur.

• **Service management system:** Perform configuration and light customization of the system. As system administrator, update user profiles, add new users, delete users, etc. Automate reporting and ensure that reports are delivered to appropriate managers on a daily, weekly and monthly basis; create new reports as needed.

• **Automatic call distribution:** Project lead for implementation of new features or upgrades. As system administrator, update user profiles, add new users, delete users, etc. Automate reporting and ensure that reports are delivered to appropriate managers on a daily, weekly and monthly basis; create new reports as needed.

• **Knowledge base:** Perform configuration and light customization of the system. Perform system administrator duties for the kb. Automate reporting and ensure that reports are delivered to appropriate managers on a daily, weekly and monthly basis.

• **Reporting:** With support center manager, design reports that integrate data from all systems. Create reports using an appropriate report-writing tool. Automate reporting and ensure that reports are delivered to appropriate managers on a daily, weekly and monthly basis; create new reports as needed.

- **Staffing and scheduling:** Create spreadsheets or other tools that enable scheduling analysts' on- and off-phone times. Use queuing theory methods to accurately predict needed headcount per hour of operation. Work with managers to optimize analysts' schedules. Create and run reports on schedule compliance for the group.

Requirements

- Two-plus years' corporate support or support center experience.
- Proficiency with Excel, Crystal Reports.
- Experience with ACDs, service management systems.
- Programming experience.
- Ability to manage multiple tasks and priorities, including good time-management skills.

Support Supervisor
XYZ Support Center

The Support Supervisor is responsible for the following tasks:

- **Call reviews and coaching:** Monitor live or recorded calls for each team member three-to-five times per month. Record evaluation of call on call review form, and enter into database if available. Conduct coaching sessions with each team member at least twice monthly to discuss call reviews and individual metrics scorecard. Track and assist team members along their career path.

- **Performance management:** Prepare and conduct yearly performance review on each team member, using the individual metrics scorecard, call and ticket review records, and other identified criteria.

- **Reporting:** Review daily metrics and reports to ensure that team members are performing within acceptable guidelines.

- **Training:** Coach analysts on procedures as necessary. Schedule training and register analysts for classes. Order courseware or manuals as necessary. Schedule knowledge-shares (informal training classes) regularly, plus other ongoing training sessions. Assist with new hire training.

- **ACD monitoring:** Monitor ACD queue for coverage. Ensure there is coverage at all times for heavy call loads.
- **Irate customers:** Assist with handling unsatisfied and irate customers, and communicate these issues with the support center manager.
- **Process compliance:** Review processes and procedures for compliance and accuracy.

Requirements

- Two-plus years' corporate support experience or two-plus years' experience in the IT industry.
- Two-plus years' experience in a supervisory role.
- {List technical requirements.}
- Strong verbal, written and interpersonal communication skills.
- Ability to manage multiple tasks and priorities, including good time-management skills.
- Must be flexible on shift.

Appendix C: Procedures Templates

Here is an outline of a procedures template. An example of a completed template is found below.

Name of procedure

Do this when

Who is involved

Dependencies (meaning, is this process invoked only after some other processes are completed?)

Process monitor and escalation

Flowchart of procedure

Description of procedure

Suggested wording

Example of procedures documentation:

Name of procedure:

Escalation from first to second-level within contact center

Do this when:

The frontline analyst has taken a call or email and has consulted with a second-level analyst who suggests escalation, or has spent 15 minutes with the customer and can't resolve the support request in another five minutes.

Who is involved:

First- and second-level analysts in contact center.

Dependencies:

Call handling procedures, especially checking all online knowledge resources, including release notes and tech notes.

Process monitor and escalation:

All analysts will work toward compliance with this procedure or will initiate a process change; managers will monitor compliance through call monitoring.

Flowchart of procedure:

{Insert flowchart of your procedure}

Step-by-step description of procedure:

The frontline analyst works the call, following normal procedures that include documenting the call, accessing the knowledge base and linking the knowledge base entry to the case, etc. If after accessing the knowledge base the analyst is still unsure how to resolve the issue, he will contact the second-level analyst(s). The second-level analyst will do one of three things:

1. Suggest some line of questioning and problem-solving for the frontline analyst to pursue.

2. Get on the phone with the frontline analyst and help resolve the support request.

3. Accept escalation of the call.

Also, if the frontline person has spent 15 minutes with the caller and isn't confident that she can resolve the support request in five more minutes, the call is escalated to second-level analysts in order to free the frontline analyst to take incoming requests.

The frontline analyst, when escalating to second-level, will place the caller in the queue and release the call.

Suggested wording:

"In order to expedite the handling of this issue and to get you to someone who can spend the time needed to resolve your issue, I am going to escalate this support request. I have thoroughly documented what we have talked about so the next contact center analyst will be able to pick up where we left off. Is that OK? Great, let me transfer you to that queue."

Appendix D: Recognition Forms

Catch Someone Doing Something Right!

On this day, _____, I caught _____ doing the following

awesome deed: _____

_____

_____

_____

_____ Signed: _____

Date: _____

I really appreciate what _____ *did to help a*

customer or fellow employee: _____

_____

_____

_____

_____ *Signed:* _____

Index